The Parklangley Club
A History

Roy Robson

2011

Published by Parklangley Freeholds Ltd.
    44a Wickham Way
    Beckenham
    BR3 3AF

Designed and typeset by *Office Geek*[1] in LaTeX[2]

Printed and bound by Williams Press

ISBN 978-0-9569330-0-3

Cover photograph
    Tennis players on court in front of the Parklangley clubhouse
    September 2010

Inside front cover illustration
    Artist's impression of the Parklangley Club
    thought to be circa late 1970s

---

[1] www.Office‑Geek.Co.UK (Apollo Data Ltd)

[2] *LaTeX Project Public Licence.* Thanks and acknowledgements to Donald Knuth, Leslie Lamport, CTAN (http://www.ctan.org/), et al, TeX, LaTeX 2$_\varepsilon$, pdfTeX 3.1415926-1.40.10 (TeXLive 2009/Debian)

"Very many congratulations to the Parklangley Club on achieving such a wonderful anniversary and for continuing to flourish and go from strength to strength. With every good wishes for the next 100 years!!"

Alan Mills CBE

Contents

List of Figures

Foreword

I was delighted to accept the invitation to write the foreword to our centenary book. My grandmother was a founder member, and so five generations of my family have participated in the various sporting activities of our very special club.

I, like many of you who will read this book, have enjoyed all that our club has offered, together with its vibrant social life. Many of us over the years married someone whom we met at the club, that is why I and my family, and many others that I know, are here today!

I feel sure that those who have gone before, if they were alive today, would be thrilled to know that the club is not only thriving, but is now more successful than it has ever been. Undoubtedly this has been due to some far-sighted decisions in the past, and to our present team led by Tony Beddoe.

We should be proud to be members of such a unique community sports club, that not only looks back at its past history, but also forward to serving future generations.

Peter Stotesbury
Chairman of the Directors
January 2011

Acknowledgements

Many years before I sat down and started tapping away at my computer, the kernel for this work was already in place. In the 1960s Willie Knoop had seen fit to write a book of memories covering the period from the 1930s to the 1960s, a magazine had been produced by club members outlining the club's history in 1986 and Ian Crane had catalogued all club tennis tournament results from 1911 to 1983. Without these works my research would have proved far more difficult.

During the course of said research I have had the pleasure of listening to the reminiscences of club members past and present whose stories and anecdotes have added force and conviction to the story. All such contributions have been greatly appreciated as without them, quite clearly, the writing of this book would have been impossible.

For his tireless efforts in garnering information on my behalf, for reviewing, editing, photographing and providing more support and assistance than I could possibly have hoped for I would like to thank Alan Whitehead.

For affording me their time and sharing their personal memories I would like to thank, in no particular order; Diana Stotesbury, Peter Stotesbury, Ian Crane, Tony Beddoe, Mark Sheldon, Dave Ash, Ron Swash, Bill Diggens, Wendy Richardson, Chris Merrick, Pam Robson, Peter Williams and many others, too numerous to name here, who have been kind enough to talk to me about their time at the club.

In an undertaking of this nature providing the words is only part of the effort, and there are many who have helped to lighten the load in putting together the final product. For their help in various forms including researching, reviewing, scanning, photographing and formatting I am grateful to Caroline Riley, Zena Wisdom, Jenny Golding, Helen Beddoe, Katarina Botkova and Simon Trice.

Artwork has never been my personal forte and when I decided the book would benefit from a cartoon or two the club again found someone with the necessary skills; for his draughtsmanship and efforts in drawing the pictures I am indebted to Tony Tidy.

This book has in effect been put together by amateurs — not in the sense that we are all hopeless but rather in that it is not what we usually do — and has taken almost two years to bring the project to fruition. Before going to print we needed it to be subject to the appropriate level of professional typesetting and formatting and for this, and his excellent additional editing, my thanks go to Alan Cumbers.

My gratitude also goes to the Parklangley Centenary Committee for having enough faith to allow me the honour of writing this short history and in particular to Julie Fox for her gentle approach to project managing me and for her ability to simply get things done.

And last, but of course no means least, I would like to express my love and thanks to my wife Pam, and my two daughters Charlotte and Danielle, for having the good grace to appreciate the fact that I had to expend significant amounts of time and energy locked away in our small office.

Roy Robson
April 2011

Introduction

One of the most salient points about my desire to write this book is that, having been a member of more sports clubs than I can now remember, the Parklangley Club is the only one for which I could ever consider such an undertaking. It is also possibly one of the few clubs I know of whose members — at least a few, I hope — will be interested in investing a little time in reading a book on its history. The club, from humble beginnings and a few dozen members, has grown to become one of the most successful sports clubs in the area, having achieved its maximum level of membership at the time of writing. Its low attrition rate is the envy of many of the lavishly funded but impersonal corporate clubs that dominate today's leisure market and its success stands as a shining example of what can be achieved by local people, working at a local level. From its very beginnings Parklangley was a club that was, and remains, deeply rooted in its local community, and it's that relationship which, for me, makes it an appealing subject for a history book.

My initial fear was that there would be insufficient material, or indeed people available, to garner enough information for a fully rounded and comprehensive history. In fact the opposite proved true. The number of people willing to help, and share their memories, has been a source of great inspiration to me. The amount of information available was at times overwhelming, and I often felt that I needed a group of research assistants to plough through it all. I quickly realised that, for an undertaking of this nature, 90% of the effort is in the research and, if this short book seems a small offering for two years of effort, my only defence is that the long hours spent reading old documents and minutes from a hundred years of AGMs — many of which revealed little of sufficient interest to include

in this book — took up most of my available time. Furthermore many
of the older management minutes were written by those who clearly had
never studied calligraphy, and proved all but impenetrable. If at some
future date an enterprising young person with infinite patience wishes to
attempt to decipher their secrets I am sure those minutes have far more
to reveal.

As a members' club Parklangley, from its earliest days, has relied on the
goodwill of an army of volunteers, that is its members, and has been in-
fused with an ethos of public spirited self-reliance — what philosopher
Edmund Burke called the 'little platoons' who exist in every corner of
British society, quietly and diligently going about their business. I had
thought that this ethos was in decline, or had perhaps fled from the Parklangley Club as it has become larger and more successful. Indeed, one
of the purposes of this book is to explore that relationship between the
club and its members, which has altered with the demands of the modern world, necessarily engendering a more professional approach. I would
suggest, however, that the original ethos still exists, at least in part, in
this little corner of Beckenham. For one need only scratch the surface to
reveal a significant number of people, such as committee members, club
captains, team captains, etc who work tirelessly away, helping to make
this club what it is.

Another concern I had was that the book would become centred on the
modern era, for the obvious reason that recent material exists in abun-
dance. I have tried my best to remedy this by concentrating research
on the pre war years, although material for this era was so sparse that
I have not been entirely successful in this particular ambition. Nevertheless, I am indebted to those who went before who saw fit to record some
of the details of those times, particularly to Mr W. and Mrs D. Knoop,
a couple who loom large over the club's early history and who feature
significantly in this book.

One of the questions that vexed me most early on was how to organise the
narrative of a hundred years of history. Veering from an initial decision
of describing everything in a straight sequential timeline, to presenting
the entire book as a selection of different topics, I eventually settled on
something between the two. The first chapter takes a brief look at the

history of the area in which the club is located, in order to set everything in context, and is followed by a light hearted look at how the club is currently constituted. The next two chapters begin the narrative from the inception of the club up to the aftermath of the Second World War. The subsequent three chapters are topic-based and can be dipped in and out of at will, before we return to the narrative in the next few chapters. The last chapter pontificates on where the club is headed and speculates on what the next hundred years might bring.

Finally, this book may be the history of a club but its essential purpose is to talk about the history of ordinary people doing ordinary things. As such my primary intention is to praise those whose effort and commitment have made the club the success that it is today, and for that I make no excuses. Time dictates that it is not possible to research every detail and capture the experience of the many hundreds, indeed thousands, who have made a contribution to the club over the last one hundred years; however, if this book contains any historical errors or glaring omissions then the responsibility is mine and mine alone.

Roy Robson
March 2011

One Hundred Years Ago – 1911

Chapter 1

Pre History

Beckenham and West Wickham

You may be wondering why a book about the history of the Parklangley Club should include a section on the history of the surrounding area and, to be fair, I have thought about removing it on several occasions. However it does, I think, help to place the club in its geographical and historical context. I lay claim to no new or insightful research, for what follows in this section is but a simple summary of the painstaking work of others far more learned than I. In particular I am indebted to the efforts of H. Rob Copeland, and his highly detailed and comprehensive 'The village of Old Beckenham', to Simon Finch's 'Images of London – Beckenham and West Wickham' and to the eminently readable 'The History of Langley Park Golf Club' by Alistair Macdonald. All of these books, and many others, provide a far more detailed picture of Beckenham's history for those among us with the time or inclination to take an interest. It is worth noting that history throws up many debates and there is always disagreement between historians regarding historical truth but, as far as I am able, I have tried to ensure that the detail here reflects only the latest thinking. What follows, then, is not an exhaustive or authoritative history but it does have one overriding advantage, which is that I have kept it mercifully short.

The long accepted and, in my experience, still prevailing truism that the name of Beckenham was derived from the Saxon 'BECC' and 'HAM' meaning a stream and a village has long since been disproved. After much painstaking — and, I'm sure, painful — research, serious historians have convinced themselves that it's actually the other way round, and that the River Beck is, in fact, derived from the village name of Beckenham. The village is referred to by various names such as BEOHHAHEMA in Charters of the 9th and 10th centuries and is probably named after Beohha, thought to be a Saxon landowner. Using our advanced powers of linguistic deduction we can take this to mean something like Beohha's settlement, or enclosure. The village name also appears in the Doomsday book around 1089, as 'BECHEHAM' and in a later reference as 'BACHEHAM'. By the way, as an aside with absolutely nothing whatsoever to do with this book, did you know that the name Domesday comes from the old English word *Dom* meaning accounting or reckoning, literally a day of reckoning. Amazing what you can quickly find on Wikipedia. Now, where was I? Oh yes, Beckenham. Well, many centuries and spelling variations later everyone appears to have agreed on the present day spelling during the 17th and 18th centuries, so let's thank our lucky stars for that.

Despite the occasional relic from the bronze and iron ages, not much information on Beckenham is available before the Romans came. Druidic worship was still practised here when they arrived and it has been speculated that the oak groves on Wickham Common are still arranged as the points of old open-air temples. Reports that the Parklangley Club is now the local centre of druid worship are largely unfounded, despite the strange incantations heard emanating from meetings of the management committee.

One hesitates to ask the question 'So what did the Romans do for Parklangley' but, of course, they left their own historical mark on the British landscape in the form of their roads. It has been established that a Roman Road passed through Beckenham in a direct line from Lower Sydenham via Langley and thence out to Titsey and Sussex, and was built to provide for the transportation of iron ore from the Sussex iron mines. It entered Beckenham near the present site of Greycot Road, crossing Bromley Road close to the site of Beckenham Theatre. Running to the west of Wickham Road and the Parklangley Club it went through the Langley Court estate and thence the golf course and into West Wickham, where it crossed the north end of Hawes Lane, Glebe Way and Corkscrew Hill. Although much of this is inferred from various ancient reference points, in the early 1930s excavations on the golf course were undertaken to confirm the physical location of the road.

Notwithstanding Roman ingenuity the district in the far off ages before tennis, squash or badminton had been invented was one of picturesque landscapes, with streams, forests and small settlements sustained by fishing and hunting the abundant wildlife that included bears, wild cats and red deer. The detail of the change from villages of scattered settlements to a borough is long, and I have promised to keep this short so it's time for a great leap forward.

Altering little since medieval times, the arrival of the railways in 1857 was the catalyst for change in the area as villa style houses started to appear around Beckenham Junction station. These soon spread as the Cator family, major landowners in the area for generations, started to release much of the land for development. Initially insisting on large houses to attract the wealthier classes (well, this is Beckenham) they later allowed smaller housing to dominate in certain areas, such as Clock House. As the town grew Beckenham applied for and became a borough in 1935, on condition that its little cousin, West Wickham, also be included.

Fig. 1.1 *Hop pickers, 1870. The Langley Estate was still surrounded by countryside at this date.*

The railway arrived at West Wickham in 1882 and, although development was slow at first, by the 1920s West Wickham, like Beckenham before it, had effectively become a London suburb.

Langley

Early historians erroneously recorded that Beckenham was divided into four manors: Beckenham, Foxgrove, Langley and Kelsey but, being early historians, perhaps they were not too good at history as apparently Langley and Kelsey were never manors but developed later as estates. The early Langley estate was said to be an extensive and rambling area from Hayes Lane up to Pickhurst and across to Eden Park and Elmers End. The theory that Langley was referred to in the Domesday book has also been discounted but, soon after the battle of Hastings, much of Kent, including Langley, was granted by William the Conqueror to his half brother Odo, Bishop of Bayeux (I wish I had relations like that).

The earliest reference to Langley in its current position is a land transfer deed from the era of Henry III (1216–1272), which was witnessed by Ralph, Richard, Henry and John de Langley, who purchased the land from the Malmains family and probably bequeathed to us their name, although the name was not adopted until some time later.

Now pay attention please as there are a lot of facts coming up. I will not be testing you so no need to remember them, and I'm going to try and do this as quickly and painlessly as possible, but please take note of some of the names for future reference. The Langley family occupied the land until 1452 when, on the death of Ralph, the last of the Langleys, they sold it to John Violet, whose family sold it on to Sir John Style in 1510. He passed it on to his son Humphrey, who was knighted in 1544, who passed it on to his son, Edmund. On Edmund's death in 1606 it went to his son William and thence to his son, another Humphrey, who was a Baronet. Humphrey had no heirs so was succeeded by his half brother William who died in 1679. The last Style to inherit the estate was Elizabeth in 1718. After her husband's death in 1729 the estate was purchased by Hugh Raymond, a director of the South Sea Company, for £26,500, eventually succeeded by his daughter Amy (whose husband was Sir John Elwill of Exeter) after the death of her brother Jones Raymond.

On her death in 1789 the estate went to her grandson, Sir Peter Burrell, who was created Lord Gwydir in 1796. On his death in 1820 the whole of his considerable Beckenham estate, which consisted of 3202 acres, was divided up and auctioned off. It extended from Monks Orchard and Ham Farm in the south, beyond Elmers End in the west, to Beckenham High Street in the north and Bromley in the east. The agents described the Langley area as *"...of the first respectability and the situation particularly desirable for a nobleman fond of hunting and shooting. It contains 423 acres and a herd of deer"*, to which one can only add that the art of the estate agent has changed little over the ensuing centuries.

Emanuel Goodhart purchased the property and it remained in the family until 1903/04 when it was further divided up and sold as building land, after the death of his son, Charles Goodhart. After the Goodharts put the area up for sale it took a full 30 years for the entire estate to be sold, with development beginning in fits and starts. By 1908 much of it was in the hands of development company H & G

Fig. 1.2 *George and Charles Goodhart – on Charles' death the estate was sold for building land.*

Taylor of Lewisham (more of them later) which bought a sizeable section of the estate and developed the golf course in 1909/10, and over the ensuing years Park Langley took on the appearance we see today. Now, if you had been paying attention when I asked, you would have noticed that one has to take but a cursory look around the area to see the landmarks many of these owners have left: Malmains Way, Styles Way, Elwill Way, Raymond Road, Burrell Close, Gwydyr Road, Goodhart Way and, of course, Langley in its many locations.

Fig. 1.3 *Park Langley or 'Chinese' Garage c. 1926. Built by Taylor's in the 1920s. The oriental style is thought to have resulted from a competition to find original designs for filling stations.*

Fig. 1.4 *Brabourne Rise under construction c. 1926. In 1908 H. and G. Taylor of Lewisham purchased a substantial section of the Langley Estate and commenced the construction of the Park Langley estate.*

Chapter 2

An Intelligent Person's Guide to the Parklangley Constitution

In 1787 James Madison drafted the document that was to form the basis of The Constitution of the United States of America, considered by many historians and constitutional experts to be one of the most important documents in history, forming the foundation on which the growth of a superpower was built. Roughly two hundred years later Alan Whitehead and Ian Crane drafted the Parklangley Constitution which, although perhaps not quite as well known, has proved equally adept at ensuring the ongoing growth and success of the club — but, although we remain hopeful, the chances of turning Parklangley into a superpower remain remote.

Now, with this in mind, during those endless hours of drizzle, rain and snow, when you are sitting at home with nothing to do and your mind is wandering all over the place, have you ever wondered about exactly how Parklangley is constituted? Speculated on exactly who owns the Club? Ruminated on how decisions are taken and, indeed, how the infinite chaos is organised? Somehow I doubt it, but nevertheless, this section is for those of you who would dare admit to such wasteful cogitation.

The club has had a myriad constitutions, names and methods of ownership over the years and we will attempt to enumerate many of these later. But

Fig. 2.1 *The Parklangley Constitution by Tony Tidy*

for now all we need to know is that by 1974 there were two separate organisations, Parklangley Freeholds Ltd (formed to hold the freehold to the land) and the Parklangley Club. In 2004 the two merged into a single organisation, Parklangley Freeholds Ltd, trading as the Parklangley Club. This new organisation took with it many of the rules of the 1974 club and enhanced them to include additional safeguards, as provided for in the Finance Act of 2002. The current Articles of Association are the result of these changes and this section merely describes, without reference to legal jargon, how the club is now constituted.

The American constitution famously begins with the words 'We the people', leaving no doubt as to where ultimate authority lies. The Parklangley constitution has few such rhetorical flourishes but, nevertheless, likewise attempts to ensure that supremacy resides with its members. The club is owned by 'Parklangley Freeholds Ltd', a company whose principal aim is the provision of amateur sporting facilities and social activities; it is registered as a community amateur sports club, and is entirely owned by its members. This immediately brings to mind two interesting questions for any member: a) 'if I own the club do I have access to any share of its profits?', and b) 'if the club were to experience any financial difficulties to what extent am I liable?'.

Unfortunately, the constitution strictly forbids even a penny from being distributed to any member, unless they happen to also be a paid employee or to have made a loan to the club, repayment of which, you will be pleased to know, is acceptable. Even if the club were wound up or became so indebted it had to be sold, and there were remaining funds available after all debts had been paid, no member can benefit. Instead, the grounds or remaining funds must be given to another amateur sports club, sports governing body or a registered charity.

On the liability side, however, you may not be so fortunate, as when a member signs on the dotted line they are signing up to limited liability for the club's debts, should the club ever experience financial difficulties. This need not give you too many sleepless nights, as the liability is limited to a maximum of fifty pence per person. So just make sure you keep your piggy bank topped up.

Structure

Essentially the club has 3 sections: Badminton, Lawn Tennis and Squash Racquets & Racquetball. Each has a committee of between 4 and 10 people, who run their own AGMs at which committee members are elected. A representative from each of these three committees sits on the Management Committee, along with six other luminaries: a Chairman, Grounds Chairman, Bar Chairman, Premises Chairman, Legal Adviser and a Financial Executive. The club manager sits as a non-voting member. Above the management committee sits the Board of Directors and provision is also made for a Disciplinary Committee to be established, as and when necessary, to deal with those of us with a tendency to stray from the straight and narrow.

This constitution underlies the authority and workings of the club just as the constitution of America is the foundation of all legal authority underpinning the country's existence. The American constitution has, broadly, four main articles which distribute power and responsibility across the country. Unbelievably, the structure of the Parklangley constitution mirrors this distribution of powers, and it is perhaps not unreasonable to say that the legendary figures who drafted it showed similar wisdom, foresight and presence of mind. Now, you may think I'm pushing the analogy a bit too far here but bear with me a little and I'll explain.

Article 1 gives the power to the legislature to make new laws, in the shape of the Senate and House of Representatives. If this isn't a highfalutin management committee I'd like to know what is. Article 2 describes the executive powers of the President, although such powers are not in the hands of a single person at Parklangley, as a safeguard against the emergence of the kind of tyrannical dictatorships that have so often disfigured community amateur sports clubs in the past. The Executive authority resides with the 'Board of Directors', although I'm not suggesting the scope of their powers or ability to apply leverage against Iran are quite as extensive as those of the President of the United States. It must be said that the Board of Directors rarely meet and, when they do, usually seek to do no more than comfort themselves that the club is rolling on more or less ok and is not menaced with any imminent threat or danger that may undermine its existence.

As far as legal issues are concerned, article 3 describes the court system, the levels of judgement each type of court is allowed to make and creates the right to trial by jury, which is to say a Parklangley member has the right to be heard by the disciplinary committee. Scary as this prospect may be, it is well to bear in mind that the law abiding member has nothing to fear if they have done nothing wrong. Rumours of a Board of Director's covert plan to build a holding/processing centre on the model of Guantamo Bay for the most difficult cases is just that, a rumour. Parklangley remains fully committed to its constitutional principles in this area.

Finally, article 4 explains the split of power and the federal relationship between the States and the central government. Stay with me on this because the comparison may be getting a bit tenuous, but doesn't the Parklangley constitution also do this by devolving powers from the management committee to the sections? Truly, a federal setup.

So there you have it. Some of the comparisons above may be ever-so-slightly facetious but underlying the frivolity are some serious points. Parklangley is organised, managed and to a great extent protected by a constitution that ensures the club can feel confident of its future, free from attack by carpetbaggers or land developers in an area where land costs are surely amongst some of the highest in the country. And I, as a long standing club member, am extremely grateful to those with the presence of mind and foresight to have established such a legacy for all those people in the area who gain great pleasure from their sporting activity.

Chapter 3

Early Years

In the Beginning

From its earliest days and until quite recently the Parklangley Club has been a club that, despite its prosperous location, has never had large sums of money to play with. Being a private members club has meant that there has never been any influx of significant share capital, nor any major corporate investment. There have been times during the last 100 years when it could barely sustain itself, and yet it has somehow always managed to survive. One way or another it has been able to obtain the necessary investment, to appoint the right person at the right time and to provide the right mix of sporting and leisure facilities that people have demanded in a changing world. Often criticised for being slow to change, it has changed when it needed to and its survival is testament to the energy, commitment and ingenuity that so many have provided across the decades.

Information on the foundation of the club is sketchy. In 1910 the whole of the Parklangley Estate was owned by H & G Taylor, a company which set about promoting its advantages with some vigour. Their general marketing efforts were clearly proving successful as, early in January of 1910, the Beckenham Journal reported that '150 applications for particulars had been received by the secretary, Mr. Frank Hudson.'

Given that the population at the turn of the century in Beckenham was no more than 27,000, they were clearly having some success. H & G Taylor developed the Langley Park Golf course in 1910 and the tennis club was another part of their original plan to promote and sell property in the area. A brochure entitled 'Ideal Homes at Parklangley, Beckenham, Kent', produced in 1910, explains the aspirations that drove the owners:

> Before determining upon the purchase of the Estate upon which their scheme was to be carried out, Messrs. H. & G. Taylor, the owners, made an exhaustive survey of the outskirts of London with a view to the discovery of beauty spots. They studied time-tables; they considered the natural amenities of districts, the easy walks from the different places under consideration, and so forth. Further they determined that each purchaser or tenant should, with his house, possess a large garden, let us say a garden with a fifty foot frontage and a depth of 200 feet. This was a very difficult task, as the price of choice land was high, and nothing but the best would suffice.

> To cut a long story short, which was long in the compiling, the Parklangley Estate was at length acquired — in all some 700 acres.

The brochure discusses the detail of the golf course at length but revealingly also contains the first known written reference to the sports club, which it describes as follows:

> TENNIS COURTS, CROQUET LAWNS, BOWLS, BADMINTON

> Some nine tennis courts have been laid down, and are in splendid condition for the 1911 season. There is ample room for more, and they will be prepared as and when required. And already a club is in the course of formation.

Four brothers who went by the name of Taylor — Henry, John, Alfred and George — are generally credited as the driving force behind the foundation of the club, and are mentioned in early records for their many services rendered. Although there is no direct documentary evidence to prove the link, it is most likely that two of the four brothers, Henry and George, were indeed the proprietors of H & G Taylor, the company that owned the estate.

When they set up the club they initially laid down 9 grass courts for Lawn Tennis, which were built on fields called 'Cross Field' and 'The Hides'. They were not all of regulation size, and three were laid at different heights, in a stepped formation. But a subscription of a mere 1 guinea which, in today's money, equates approximately to an inflation busting £90 would, no doubt, have helped to make amends for the fact that the court dimensions were somewhat irregular.

Eager residents of the recently built estate proved to be enthusiastic about their new club and swiftly moved to form the Parklangley Sports Club in 1911, when the first Honorary Secretary, Mr. E. Fermin, was also appointed. Although there is little documentary evidence available to pinpoint exactly when and for how much, by 1911 ownership of the land had passed to London and Kent Estates. Furthermore, the first formally agreed contract with the landowners was signed that same year, when the Parklangley Sports Club arranged a 28 year lease for exclusive usage of the land. This is a significant moment as it guarantees that the land cannot be used for further development and embeds the idea of a sustainable sports and social club within the Langley estate.

The next year the 'temporary' Badminton Hall was built, with the Badminton Club also starting in 1912. It was a building — well, at least a structure of some kind — that, over the course of the following century, was to take on a near legendary status, surviving fire, floods, bombs and other general biblical visitations of plague and pestilence. Architecturally one would hesitate to call it beautiful but it did have a certain character, and over the years developed a personality of its own. It might have been cheap, small and cold, and you had to be very careful not to hit a shuttlecock too high or else it would re-bound off the beams, but it somehow reflected the spirit of the club in the years before the modern world inevitably brought about its demise. It was, in actuality, used for a multitude of sporting and social activities and those members who have been around for a while remember it, rather like an old friend, with fondness and some sentimentality, even though we may look back through rose

Fig. 3.1 *Old Badminton Hall – The ninety year old 'temporary' bad-minton hall, built c. 1912 — here seen in a sorry state of repair — held wonderful memories for many members and was the focal point of many club activities including dinners, dances, revues, quizzes, aer-obics, gymnastics, physiotherapy and, whenever they could manage to fit it in, badminton.*

tinted glasses. For many years the club had to apply to the local coun-cil for a bi-annual licence, to ensure that badminton could continue to be played. In the end, however, the hall somehow managed to out-manoeuvre the long arm of bureaucracy, the authorities eventually throwing in the towel as inspections petered out. The hall was finally knocked down in 2001, to make way for the current clubhouse, having extended the usage of the word temporary somewhat beyond its standard dictionary definition.

During those early years, with the club and its facilities now in place, it was visited by a reporter from the Beckenham and Penge & Sydenham Advertiser. In an article of July 8th 1911 he describes the first annual tournament of the Parklangley Tennis Club. It is a wonderfully expressive and timely article which captures some of the spirit and observance of the social niceties prevalent at the start of the 20th century. It is the earliest known writing concerning the activities of club members and is re-produced here in full:

LAWN TENNIS CLUB FESTIVAL

Last week our eyes were attracted by a neatly designed notice outside the Parklangley Estate Office, announcing that the first annual tournament of the Parklangley Tennis Club would take place on July 1st, and would be followed by an Alfresco Entertainment. We had already heard of the great success of the club which although only a few months old, boasts of close upon 100 members and obtaining a close view of their habitat and festivities, found that the tournament was being run on the American principle where each couple plays every other, and the scoring was by the actual number of strokes won. It was odd too to hear such cries of scores at "nine – eleven, change serve, eleven – nine".

We did not profess to understand, but concluded that on the Estate the mathematical faculties are even more highly developed than are the tennis faculties. This conclusion was strengthened when on inspecting the scoring sheet at the end of play, we found that the handicapping committee had so accurately gauged the intricacies of the figures that the pairs were 2 all in a bunch separated by remarkably few points.

Once during the course of the afternoon our nerves were jarred by the shrill whistle of the photographer, but we pretended to misunderstand his wishes and make a dash for the pavilion where tea was on the point of being served, such an excellent tea too, for the lady members have taken upon themselves the duty of seeing that they get a good tea by the simple expedient of providing it themselves, and the caterer of some clubs is at Parklangley replaced by a rota of lady members.

The clerk of the weather had evidently been squared, for he doled out of his best. Indeed the tennis Club Committee, who were giving the entertainment are to be congratulated on getting on the blind side of everyone.

They were particularly fortunate in enlisting the support of Mr. West, a resident, and inducing him to arrange and stage-manage their musical programme. The first thing to attract our attention even before we reached the ground was the wealth of the illuminations. The pavilion itself outlined with electric light, was under the blaze of a huge southern cross, also in electric light. The whole of the ground, which comprises nine courts, was decked around with fairy lamps and Chinese lanterns, while the stage in addition to its floral decorations displayed in cunning arrangement every form of illumination. The company must have been a good two hundred strong, and might well have been more had the gathering been advertised. One indeed would have put the estimate higher had one judged solely by the volume of laughter 'at $9\frac{1}{2}$ an hour' or the peals of clapping from the two little hearts that beat as one Mr. West had been fortunate enough to secure the services of the well-known Stradella Company, and thus ensured the success of the concert. Mr. Inglefield, another resident on the estate, was also kind enough to give his services, and delighted the gathering with some fine renderings of well-known songs.

Just before the interval the Hon. Secretary, in the name of the committee, welcomed the gathering and proposed a vote of thanks to the Stradella Company, and personally to each of those who had helped the committee to arrange and carry out the entertainment. He suggested that the interval should be spent in strolling peaceably around the site of that afternoon's battleground.

The second half of the programme requires no special mention other than it was as good as the first, and that nearly every item was encored.

At eleven o'clock sharp the curtain rang down, and valsing on courts became the order of the day, but a couple of good long valses on dewy grass takes a good deal out of one, so we all gathered around the pavilion again to sing the National Anthem and give a few last hearty cheers before dispersing. As all trooped off the ground a remark was made which found an echo in many hearts: "Well, here endeth the first Tennis Club Entertainment, but I jolly well hope it won't be the last."

One hundred years later we can safely say that the person responsible for those last words has most definitely got his wish.

In these early days membership was made up almost exclusively of residents of the estate, with outside members being rare. Apart from a few tantalising snippets of information here and there not much is known of the early years of the club, or how it was structured and managed. Its progress, of course, was profoundly interrupted by the Great War, when lots of prospective players must have been lost to that awful conflict and, indeed, the scarcity of players was felt for many years afterwards. It was a time when reports of local tennis clubs often appeared in local papers but Parklangley appeared to be an exception, appearing only fleetingly, for instance in the reports of a match played at an opposing club. Whether the unfortunate occurrence of keeping the club a closely guarded secret was the result of deliberate intent or simply a matter of indifference we will probably never know. However, thanks to the painstaking investigative work of Ian Crane, which is published in his booklet 'Parklangley Tennis Club Tournaments up to 1983', we do have a reasonable picture of the winners and runners up for a significant number of early competitions. Ian's is a work of unparalleled detail, and one that I do not hope or aspire to replicate here, and tells us that — despite the war — the first formally recorded club tennis championships were still held in 1914, when the men's singles title went to Mr R H Hurlbat and the ladies to Mrs E Davy whose grandson, Peter Stotesbury, at the time of writing, remains on the club's Board of Directors and Management Committee.

The club's earliest known inter-club match was a friendly against Beckenham Cricket Club in 1912. Despite a valiant effort it was reported that Parklangley lost 8–1. The earliest record of a Parklangley winning team was a 5–4 victory over Albemarle Lawn Tennis Club in 1914.

Given the paucity of information available to us we must now jump forward to 1919, when, as far as we are aware, the second club tournament was held with the men's singles title going to Mr R Ingram and the women's to Mrs Chadwick. But the year is also a significant date in the club's history for far more sober reasons. It was the year when the club experienced the first of its many financial emergencies when it became apparent that the Taylor brothers had originally over extended themselves. It has been suggested that their plans for the club were perhaps too ambitious, for instance they had held illusions of a very grandiose club house that never came to fruition. The detailed club finances of the period are unavailable but the upshot is that, if the club was to survive, the members had to intercede in club affairs and provide private funding. It was the first time that club members were called upon to ensure the club remained financially viable and, over the next century, would prove to be far from the last. They thought highly enough of their club to allow me a flourish of clichés as they bit the bullet, put their money where their mouths were and put their hands in their pockets to come up with the necessary. And thus it came to pass that the club acquired formal legal status with its registration as The Parklangley Sports Club Limited, under the chairmanship of W. F. Crutch, on the 16th of April 1919. Registered with a capital of £500, 15 members took up original share ownership. These, for the sake of posterity, are recorded below:

> Edward North, Edgar Fraser, Herbert Cubitt, Albert Carman, Walter Wolsey, Arthur Cleveland, Cecil Howard, Stephen Saldi, John Crutch, William Crutch, James Davis, James McCaffery, Arthur Lewis, Richard Crittall, William Smith.

The company was set up as a 'Private Company', in the sense that no members of the public could apply for shares, and share ownership was entirely controlled by the Board. Only club members were allowed to purchase shares, no one person could take ownership of more than 50 and any transfers required the previous written sanction of the directors. The Board initially consisted of 5 directors:

> William George Smith of 23 Wickham Way
> Richard Godfrey Crittall of 49 Wickham Way
> William Henry Tapp of 88 Wickham Way
> James McCaffery of 3 Elwill Way
> William Fredrick Crutch of 32 Wickam Way

Many members followed the original 14 subscribers as share ownership increased steadily. In consequence, as the ravages of the First World War started to fade into memory, the club was in reasonable shape, financially secure, now playing regular tournaments and having survived the first of its many financial crises. Indeed by 1926, 371 shares had been taken up, and this had increased to 390 by 1930.

Steady Progress

The second decade of the club's life witnessed the societal upheaval known as the Roaring Twenties, which began in North America and spread to Europe in the aftermath of the First World War. Europe spent these years rebuilding and coming to terms with the vast human cost of the conflict, but by the middle of the decade economic development soared, and the second half of the decade became known as the 'Golden Twenties'. The automobile became a common means of transport, new modern devices found their way into homes, and people had more free time on their hands than ever before. So with this free time many turned their attention to sports. Interest in tennis soared and by the 1920s Wimbledon had become the world's most important tennis championship, moving to its current location in 1922.

Meanwhile in a little corner of Beckenham the Parklangley Club continued to make steady progress. From what limited information is available it appears that the club prospered, at least to the extent that most tennis clubs prospered. In 1921 the Club was affiliated to the Kent County Lawn Tennis Association. A further 3 shale courts were laid down in 1925, making winter tennis possible for the first time, and the ground rent went up to a staggering £20 per annum.

In 1924 W. Knoop — whose affiliation with the club was to last for many years and, as we shall see, was to become an important figure in the club's history — took over as captain of the men's Tennis team and, as a sign of growing professionalism and maturity, is said to have spent many hours stalking public courts looking for promising young talent to bring to the club. This anecdote comes to us from the book of memories previously mentioned and is the first evidence we have that the club — or some members at least — had realised something simple, but rather important; if it was to survive and flourish, membership could no longer be formed exclusively from residents of the Park Langley estate.

Badminton, then as now the perennial second sport of the club, was also doing rather well during the period. The standard was unquestionably high as in 1928 Mrs Burgess Smith gained her County Colours for Kent, the first Parklangley member to have achieved such honours.

Fig. 3.2 *Parklangley Kent Cup finalists, 1931 – from left to right H. Leak, W. Knoop, A.B. McDougal (captain), J.B. Lambert, D.F. Stotesbury, L. Shiner*

But it was tennis that had captured the public's imagination and continued to increase in popularity. In the 1930s the game became highly fashionable, led by British stars such as Fred Perry and international champions such as Henri Lacoste and Don Budge. You'll notice from the photograph of the Parklangley Kent Cup Finalists of 1931 that tennis fashions were somewhat different in those days. Long trousers were the order of the day for men, and for women it was long dresses and stockings. The changing nature of sportswear simultaneously reflects both changes in the nature and intensity of the game and the profound social changes of the intervening decades. How quaint and demure this now seems to our modern sensibilities, a lost and almost alien world of simplicity and innocence, a world for which many yearn but to which none can ever return. But before we get bogged down in nostalgia it is worth recalling that even by the 1930s fashion trends had already been developing. Indeed, it is hard to believe that Britain's Bunny Austin shocked the crowds in 1933 when he became the first player to step out on to centre court wearing shorts!

Generally, the 1930s were a boom time for tennis and in 1937 the Wimbledon championship was broadcast on the radio for the first time. This was a significant event, truly introducing tennis to the world, and this interest in tennis was reflected in the continuing steady progress at Parklangley. The decade saw some significant advances in terms of its facilities, its sporting development and its social activities. The drive to recruit some promising young players paid off as tennis membership, for all categories, rose to 166 by 1931, 188 by 1932 and 211 by 1934. Competition for courts forced the management committee into setting an upper limit of 130 on players eligible to play on Saturdays and Sundays. This increase in membership allowed the club to enter more teams into the Kent Cup competitions. A Parklangley team played in the final of the Kent Junior Cup on the 25th July 1931 and in 1934 the men's first team made the final of the intermediate section of the Kent Cup, the first occasion any senior Parklangley team had ever reached a Kent final, losing to Private Banks II.

Although the early 1930s had seen successful fund raising activities which allowed for extensions to the bar area, it was often mentioned that in those days the changing facilities remained somewhat primordial and drainage, in particular, is often cited as the cause of some distress. An improvement fund was established in 1930 which brought in an astounding £38. The club continued to be well run, in terms of expenditure control at least, with the accounts of 1931 improving from the previous year's £61 loss to a £3 profit thanks largely, according to the accounts of the period, to "*the strictest economy of expenditure*". The accounts that year also noted that "*further expansion of the number of members of the Tennis Club is necessary if the club is to be carried on*". To this end, using the improvement fund and negotiating extra funds from the landlords, the changing facilities were improved and some work was carried out on the 'temporary' badminton hall — well, it did last almost 100 years so someone had to keep it going.

The Great Depression seems to have had little or no impact on the general progress and finances of the club as small improvements continued. The hard courts were resurfaced in 1933 and 1937, and by 1939 the problem of the primordial nature of the changing rooms was finally resolved when new brick facilities were built, and the clubhouse was also further improved.

Fig. 3.3 Outside the tennis courts, June 1941 – ⟨unknown⟩, H.D. MacKensie, M. Lund, M. Hague, D. Knoop, F. West, W. Knoop and P. Wheeler

The money was raised by an issue of debentures valued at £12 10s each, and totalling £750 pounds, of which £562 10s were subscribed in the first 8 months. This was a vast sum of money for the club, almost trebling the balance sheet value from £504 in 1937 to £1,417 in 1939. The General Committee of the Parklangley Lawn Tennis Club agreed to repay the money to the directors of the Parklangley Sports Club in a 'gentlemen's agreement between the company and the club'.

Sadly the close of the thirties bore witness to the arrival of the Second World War, and after 1939 the Wimbledon championships closed until 1946. Incidentally this was the last year at Wimbledon in which a player wore long trousers on court.

Chapter 4

The Second World War and its aftermath

We are all familiar with the idea that, in Britain, the Second World War generated a certain spirit; a camaraderie characterised by a determination not to give in; a fortitude of mind and body and a resolve — as far as was possible under the circumstances — to continue as normal. It may be difficult to say how this spirit physically displayed itself and, at the end of the day, perhaps it was just no more than an inner belief that things must go on. In 1940 at the annual general meeting of the Parklangley Lawn Tennis club, chaired by club captain Mr. Donald F. Stotesbury, that is precisely what the club did — ensured that as far as was possible it would be business as usual. The secretary, after referring to the war-time character of the meeting, was able to state that 'the support in favour of continuing the facilities for play during the coming season was very marked'. The club therefore resolved to open as usual although such things as 'matches and tournament play' could only be arranged on the spur of the moment. 'There would also be social activities'.

Despite this resolve these were, of course, tough years for club, King and country. Many members were lost to the forces, and blackout regulations after the winter of 1939 made it impossible for Badminton to be played. The combined loss of Badminton revenue and members' subscriptions meant once again that the very existence of the club was in jeopardy, for example revenues collapsed from £235 in 1940 to £188 in 1941. Once again, however, the club had the people with enough vision and commitment to ensure its ongoing survival. In 1939 the management committee of the time not only renewed the lease for a further 21 years with an option for an additional 7 years, they simultaneously arranged for the suspension of lease payments. Cometh the hour, cometh the committee, as they say. It must also be said that the landowners, London and Kent Estates Limited, were highly sympathetic to the club's plight in those desperate times, and did everything they could to aid the club in its battle for survival. Indeed, in a letter to the club in 1942 they make it quite clear that they would love to be in receipt of some rent — no doubt they were likewise desperate — but were prepared "*to accept without question the figure at which after due consideration, the Club arrives*". But perhaps most importantly of all, if we think about the long term viability and independence of the club, a clause was inserted into the agreement that allowed for the outright purchase of the freehold at some future date, without which you would almost certainly not be reading this book right now.

Having resolved to keep the club open, and having committed to running tournaments, it was time to deliver. Despite the fact that some of the courts were reserved for the growing of vegetables to help the war effort, junior tournaments were held at Parklangley in 1940, 41, 42, 43, 45 and 46. Regrettably the 1944 tournament was cancelled after the development of the V-1 or 'doodlebug' — the first of these flying bombs hit London on 12th June 1944. A total of 9,251 V-1s were fired at Britain, with the vast majority aimed at London; 2,515 actually reached the city and more fell on Beckenham than any other London borough.

Many junior tournaments during the period had the support of Mr. R. L. Quertier's, 'Junior Club of Great Britain'. Quertier was also, co-incidently, the Parklangley chairman and helped secure the support of the LTA for twinned tournaments at both Parklangley and the Northwick Lawn Tennis club in Harrow. The most famous of these tournaments was dubbed 'The Battle of Britain' Tournament, which took place during the early stages of that epoch defining encounter. It was run in aid of the Red Cross and attracted 141 competitors. Known as 'London's Junior Tennis Fortnight' the event secured the princely sum of £150 for the Red Cross — Parklangley's contribution being a highly creditable £90.

Fig. 4.1 *Poster of London's junior tennis fortnight, 1940*

The final day of the tournament was attended by the Mayor of the Borough, who witnessed a series of exhibition matches which attracted a crowd of 600 and which, according to the Evening News, *"rounded off a great week, which provided a really bright spot in dreary tennis days"*. Air raid shelters, a necessity for which we thankfully have no further need, were kindly provided for the public by The Welcome Foundation.

The first bomb to fall on Beckenham landed on 26th August 1940 in the field of the Yokohama Specie Bank in Worsley Bridge Rd (see [1] Watkins and Manning p.8) and the Luftwaffe thereafter had the courtesy to pay a personal visit to the Parklangley Club during the war, with a bomb dropping on the then court 10 — which, it is believed, is now court 3.

The visit came on the night of 1st November, 1940. All the tiles and glass in the badminton hall were smashed and metal and stones covered the remaining courts – it takes little imagination to picture the scene. The next morning Jean Quertier, Mary Wheeler, the groundsman P. J. Eades and others were recruited for the clear up operation, and by 11am that day the ladies, in a display of old fashioned British bloody mindedness, had a game of singles. Now, it was not recorded who won but as a symbolic gesture of defiance it captures, perhaps, a little of the spirit of those dark days. The bunker was not filled in until after the war but instead, in common with several of the courts, was used for growing vegetables, and became famed for the excellence of its marrows. Another beneficiary of the raid was St. Christopher's School, whose scrap metal collection is said to have expanded considerably.

Ironically it is thanks to the money made during the war, especially that generated by the junior tournaments, that the debentures were all repaid by 1946 with sufficient funds remaining to repair the bomb damage to the badminton hall, and the sport returned to the club that same year.

1945 – The Victory Tournament

The first post war tournament was known, for obvious reasons, as the Victory Tournament and again was played only for the championship of the junior club. Run in celebratory mood the tournament drew an attendance of some 1,200 people determined to enjoy themselves in post war celebration, despite the continuing shortages. It is reported that, after seven years of bombing and rationing, the shortage of tea was a particular problem and that the capacity to serve said liquid refreshment was strained to breaking point. However, reliable testament is available to the fact that over 800 teas were served on the day — agreed by all to have been a remarkable performance given the circumstances. The significance of this cannot be underestimated, for the members of Parklangley were celebrating not just a tennis tournament but a war victory, and for the British to celebrate without their tea would have been, well, not really British. Accordingly Mr Knoop gives special mention in this undertaking, in his 1961 book of memories, to the three heroines who served the tea, whose names I feel compelled once more to promote to the higher echelons of Parklangey lore: Mrs. A. J. Magrath, Mrs. D. Knoop and Mrs. Kathleen Leek.

The war and post war years, as you would expect, also saw the continuation of shortages of more or less everything and for the tennis player the shortages of tennis balls was particularly acute. These days the supply of tennis balls presents no problems, with approximately 300 million balls being produced annually. This creates roughly 14,700 metric tons of waste in the form of rubber that is not easily biodegradable, but with a little imagination we can readily discern a number of uses for them. For instance how about a pair of the oft discussed tennis ball headphones for DIY enthusiasts who do not like the sound of their drills, baby proofing a room by cutting off a small portion of the ball and fixing them to the sharp corner of your coffee table, or fixing them to the edge of a broomstick in order to clear the cobwebs from your ceiling.

With a little thought I'm sure you could think of many more but in 1944 the severe shortage of rubber meant, for the tennis enthusiast, that tennis balls were for one thing and one thing only — playing tennis. Following representations from the LTA, it was agreed in that year that tennis balls could be made of synthetic rubber, as was already the case in America. However, even then the Board of Trade allowed only minor quantities to be made available for such usage.

Consequently post war shortages continued to exist and thus the Parklangley Club had to continue doing what it had done during the war, namely re-conditioning the existing natural rubber balls. In 1946 club secretary Mr. Knoop wrote to tennis members informing them that "*Synthetic rubber having been placed at the disposal of Manufacturers by the Ministry of Supply, it will be possible next season to make a certain quantity of balls available to Lawn Tennis Clubs*", but with the amount of supply still uncertain members should "*deliver at the door not later than 15th November, such balls for reconditioning as they can spare, when I shall be pleased to do the needful on the same lines as last season*". That is, send them off to be re-conditioned.

Now, it's doubtful whether the reconditioning process restored the bounce of the ball to its former glory but at least it meant that some play could continue. It has been estimated that, in the UK, around 360,000 balls were reconditioned between April 1943 and March 1944.

In October 1945 the club, once again on a reasonably secure financial footing, resumed its full lease payments to London and Kent Estates Ltd. whose secretary, Mr. T.W. Livesey, in acknowledgement of the gesture wrote:

> *I have been filled with admiration for the activities of the Club throughout these difficult years and I offer my congratulations to those concerned in what in my opinion is a remarkable achievement.*

This is also a time that the club took on a management structure more familiar to today's members, with separate management committees for the tennis and badminton sections. The members club was renamed 'Park-langley Lawn Tennis and Badminton Club' and each section maintained a separate set of accounts with surpluses going to the 'C' account, which was used by the Limited Company to pay ongoing running costs. A new set of rules was approved to take into account the changes and, by 1947, membership subscriptions to either section were set at £3 3s, and by 1949 the accounts show that the club was full, with membership being maintained at maximum level.

The club had again emerged from a period of financial instability. It had risen to the challenge of repairing and improving its facilities during difficult times, it had made the necessary financial and organisational alterations necessary to ensure its ongoing survival and was in a position in which it could face the future with confidence. When it needed to change it had managed to find the people who understood this, and brought the change about. This change was by no means revolutionary or dramatic, but nor did it need to be, for those who managed the club through the war years intrinsically understood what was required in order for the club to continue serving its surrounding community.

Chapter 5

The famous and the not so famous

"I'm afraid of loosing my obscurity. Genuineness only thrives in the dark. Like celery", is a quote from the Aldous Huxley novel 'Those Barren Leaves', that seeks to shred the pretensions of those who would claim a place for themselves amongst celebrities. Most people who toil away behind the scenes at Parklangley rarely display such affectation, so this chapter presents a very short Parklangley biography of a few of them. Again, if I'm honest, this book is not encyclopaedic and can only represent a flavour of the many hundreds who have made significant contributions over the years.

During the first half century of the club there were undoubtedly many whose contribution was considerable, but much about them has been lost in the mists of time.

Stalwarts

Mr and Mrs Knoop

Within the history of any successful club there exists the spirit of the unsung hero, alive in those who work with dedication and commitment to ensure the organisation continues, thrives and grows. Shunning self promotion, their ethos, especially in a club such as Parklangley, is to just get on with the job. In the early years of the club two people stand out as being firmly in this category. They are Mr and Mrs Knoop.

The Knoops took on the role of joint secretaries in 1930, a position that they held for 31 years, dedicating a significant amount of their lives to ensuring that Parklangley prospered and thrived. Indeed much of the information in this book is only available because of the records they left behind, most notably the book of memories which contains a short history of the early years of the club. Mr Knoop also wrote many of the minutes of AGMs and management meetings by hand. After several frustrating attempts to decipher them I reluctantly decided that keeping my sanity was more important than interpreting his impenetrable scribble.

Mr Knoop is said to have been the dominant character and, in an age where propriety and decorum were far more important than they are now, he insisted upon correct dress code and standards of behaviour. Through 31 years the Knoops steered the club through some of the worst, the best and the most important events in the club's history. As well as administering the club and holding it together they provided reports for the local papers and their time saw many improvements to club facilities, as documented elsewhere in this book. They guided the club through the war years and were present during the momentous time, again detailed elsewhere in this book, when Donald Stotesbury, Gordon Morrish and Ralph Thompson masterminded the purchase of the freehold in 1952 which, in my view, is the single main reason the club survives to this day. In 1961, at the end of their period as honorary secretaries, the facilities were in excellent condition and the club had become a prosperous and thriving concern.

Fig. 5.1 *A youthful Mr and Mrs Knoop, May 1921*

Times were different when the Knoops ran the club and they were never paid a penny for their services. Having helped to start yet another fund raising exercise on the occasion of the club's Golden Jubilee in 1961, in a personal statement at the end of their book of memories written in 1961 the Knoops enounced on some of the things that inspired them to continue for so long, and I will leave the last words to them:

> *Too many clubs have gone to the wall because there was enjoyment without thought for the future. By the purchase of the ground a security has been created on which members can build in the future.*
>
> *We pray and hope that clubs may not have to face again war conditions and rationing, but there will always be smaller problems. This club's members over 50 years have proved that they can be mastered.*
>
> *There maybe those who have found their happiness and made friendships there. Or still others may admire what amateurs have done and may feel that the continuation of such facilities will be a good thing for a younger generation.*
>
> Mr and Mrs Knoop, 1961

Donald Stotesbury

Donald was the father of Peter who wrote the Foreword for this book, which highlights something of the intergenerational nature of the club. Donald, occasionally a controversial character, was a stalwart of the club for many decades, was tennis captain during the Second World War and continued to captain a number of tennis teams for some years after. He ensured the continuing club success when he convinced the two sections of the club to add squash courts in 1970.

He oversaw the maintenance of the grounds for many years and also represented the Club on the Council of the Kent County Lawn Tennis Association with a particular interest in Juniors.

Johnny Cridland

Johnny was an outstanding Tennis Captain and a regular member of the first team.

Bill Parkin

Bill was a stalwart of the Badminton Section, who fought for equality for the Badminton Section although its membership was much smaller than the Tennis Section.

In the second half century more is known and it is therefore inevitable that omissions may be hurtful and for these apologies may be due.

Ron Swash

Ron was another outstanding Tennis Captain who drove the move for our first floodlit tennis court and had members digging trenches for power cables and raising money for this. He was also much involved in all the Revues.

Zena Huggan (nee Urmston)

Zena was an outstanding Lady Captain of the tennis section and a regular member of the first team. She later became non-playing Ladies Captain of Kent, a position she held for many years.

Peter Stotesbury

Many Parklangley members have very long associations with the club and none more than Peter Stotesbury, who is a third generation member. His maternal grandmother, Mrs. E. Davy, was the first ever ladies tennis champion, his younger brother Michael was tennis champion several times and Peter partnered him to win the doubles on many occasions. More recently his son and three daughters have all made their mark at tennis.

Fig. 5.2 *Peter Stotesbury*

Over the years Peter has held many positions in the club including Tennis Captain, Chairman of Parklangley Freeholds, first Chairman of the Squash Section, and for many years following in his father's footsteps as Ground Chairman.

Peter also represented the club on the Kent County LTA and served as match secretary and selector for the Kent Men's Team for many years.

Alan Whitehead

Fig. 5.3 *Alan Whitehead*

Alan is another unsung hero, having provided forty years of unpaid service to the club, tirelessly toiling away to help create and maintain its ongoing success. During his time he has been both Chairman and Finance Executive, and his unseen hand has often ensured that the club has been guided in the right direction. He together with Ian Crane secured the club's future by ensuring it has a formal and legal constitution as a community amateur sports club, which prevents the club grounds being used for any other purpose than as a sports ground. During his time at the financial helm he is said to have had a very *"positive attitude to burning money"* on new projects, which is a testament to the confidence he has in the club's future.

Alan Thompson

Alan played all three sports at the club, but tennis was his first love and he seemed to get better with age winning the Singles, Men's Doubles and Mixed Doubles in 1986 at the age of 44. Right up till his death in 2009 he was playing Veterans Tennis for Kent (45 appearances) in the first division where they were runners up in 2007.

He was a Director of Parklangley Freeholds and Club Chairman from 1990 to 1994 seeing Tony Beddoe settle into the position of Club Manager.

Stan Shand

Another unsung hero, ably supported by his wife Maureen was a stalwart of the Badminton Section for many years injecting his enthusiasm all around him.

Mike Kelly

Mike has been involved in virtually every building project the club has initiated in the last 20 years. He was Project Manager for the Nissen shaped badminton hall, the indoor tennis hall, the third squash court, the new clubhouse and the latest addition the new kids room. He has been chairman of the club for the last 5 years and has been sitting on the Management Committee since the mid '80s.

Fig. 5.4 *Mike Kelly*

Fred Harbour

Fred, who had been a member for some years, took early retirement and trained as a tennis coach. He then established the first coaching programme at the club in the course of which he coached many youngsters who went onto greater things including Sally Reeves, Jenny Reeves, Michelle Wheeler, Maria Wheeler, Colin Beecher, Mark Sheldon and Kester Jackson. Fred also represented the club on the Kent LTA.

David Ash

David has been the tennis chairman for several years and has run the Junior Tournament held at the Club every Spring Bank Holiday for many years. He also represents the club on the council of the Kent LTA.

Tony Beddoe

Fig. 5.5 *Tony Beddoe*

For many Parklangley members Tony Beddoe is a legend in his own lunch hour. He has been club manager since 1990 and was chairman before that. His impact on the club has been immense and he has driven forward the Parklangley modernising agenda with unyielding determination and energy.

Mick Proffitt

Mick Proffitt is the club's longest serving employee having been appointed groundsman in the late 1980s, since when the lumps in the tennis courts have all but disappeared. He has been keeping them in mint condition for something approaching eternity.

Fig. 5.6 *Mick Proffitt*

Bill Diggens

Bill was club chairman from 1995 to 2003 during which time he took the club into the largest building project it has ever undertaken — the construction of the current clubhouse — fighting and winning a number of battles for funding for new facilities.

Players

From the club's earliest days there is evidence that many members played their sport at a high level, but there is scant evidence to suggest anybody achieved the dizzying heights of national standard until after the war.

Jean Quertier

In tennis Jean Quertier was the outstanding post war player. She played at Wimbledon several times reaching the second round in 1946, the 3rd round in 1947 and the quarter finals in both 1948 and 1952.

Fig. 5.7 Jean Quertier

Annabel Croft

Annabel Croft took up tennis when she was nine, and at 15 became the youngest Briton to play at Wimbledon for nearly 100 years. Annabel played for the Parklangley Club for around 3 years in the early seventies, which she says had a huge impact on her early tennis career. She spent her summers playing and practising against a variety of opponents with wide ranging styles which she considers gave her an excellent grounding in the sport, and remembers a wonderful few years *"drinking Robinson's squash"* whilst relaxing in the *"old fashioned club house"*.

Fig. 5.8 *Annabel Croft*

In 1984, Annabel was a Wimbledon Junior Champion and a year later picked up her first senior tournament trophy in San Diego.

Other alumni who have played at Wimbledon over the years include Sally Reeves and the doubles pairing of Jennifer MacIntosh and Judy Watts.

Badminton

Post war Badminton went from strength to strength as all first teams — Mens, Ladies and Mixed — rose to the top divisions, and all three Kent League Championships were won in 1948/49, this 'triple crown' was a first for any Kent club, a terrific achievement repeated in 49/50, 58/59, and 59/60. Not surprisingly, during this post war period, Parklangley contributed 14 players to the county Kent team, including two who would go on to be internationals, John Best and Audrey Stone.

John Best

John played for the England badminton team 44 times. Despite his international successes, however, he often failed to get selected for his university, Cambridge, being kept out of the team by foreign competition in the form of three Malayans: Choung, Choung and Choung.

Audrey Stone

The Parklangley Club's second England player achieved 3 caps for England and won the French Open in 1952.

Fig. 5.9 *John Best (on the right) after winning the men's tennis singles tournament at Parklangley, 1949*

Parklangley player's national title

VICTORY in the singles final for 18-year-old Alison Black; defeat for Alison and 16-year-old Jennifer Cridland in the doubles final. That was the outcome for the two local girls who last week-end took part in the last stages of the *Evening News* junior lawn tennis tournament at the Queen's Club.

Alison, who lives at 95d Albemarle-road, Beckenham, and Jennifer, of 55, Whitecroft-way, Parklangley, were taking part in the tournament for the first time. They are both members of Parklangley Tennis Club.

For Alison, her singles semi-final match against Miss Bonnie Atkins, which she won in three sets, was the hardest she played throughout the tournament. During the match the players had to transfer from the grass court to an indoor wood court when rain interfered.

Of her finals victory in two straight sets, Alison said her opponent, Miss Mildner, was nervous, and was never able to get into the game.

Alison was presented with the singles trophy by the L.T.A. coach, Mr. Dan Maskell.

After a three sets win in the doubles semi-finals, Alison and Jennifer went out in the final by two straight sets. They each received vouchers as a consolation prize.

Said Alison: "We had two set points in this game, but they were better than us. They were older and more experienced players."

Jennifer is this week taking part in the Kent County Junior Lawn Tennis championships in Beckenham.

But Alison told me that she does not expect to play much tennis for the remainder of this year. Earlier this year she completed a secretarial training course, and is now hoping to get a job.

Both girls have been playing doubles together for some time, and have had several successes in a number of junior tournaments in various parts of Southern England.

Jennifer Gridland (left) and Alison Black

Fig. 5.10 *Jennifer Cridland and Alison Fraser-Black, article in The Evening News, with commentary on their victory at The Queen's Club. Date uncertain.*

Chapter 6

Playtime

"We don't stop playing because we grow old; we grow old because we stop playing." said playwright and philosopher George Bernard Shaw. It is a quote that many of us can identify with and, as well as joining the club to play sport, many people join clubs such as Parklangley to enjoy some simple, old fashioned fun. This section takes a brief, haphazard and totally incomplete look at the way in which this sentiment has been expressed at the Parklangley Club across the decades.

Revues

"All the world's a stage, but the play is badly cast." — Oscar Wilde

I have mentioned before that there is something about the Parklangley Club, something that has persisted across the decades, that encourages many of its members to get involved, most especially when there are funds to be raised — which, thinking about it, is most of the time. Never has this spirit shown greater originality, inventiveness and artistic endeavour than in the early to mid sixties. It is unlikely that you would consider the Club to be the natural place for would be thespians to try their hand at treading the boards but during these times club members wrote, directed and acted in a series of Revues. Displaying an imagination for proactive pastimes that predominated before leisure time was so dominated by television, three revues were put on over a period of roughly five years.

The 1961 Revue was timed to coincide with the Club's Golden Jubilee and was entitled 'Would Jubilee Vit' whilst the Revue of 1965 was named 'Beyond the Pale'. The productions were performed in the Badminton Hall (here's yet another use for that legendary temporary structure for those of you keeping count) or at The Assembly Hall, Gates Green Road in West Wickham. Cryptic sketches included 'Hitler Never had a Chance', 'Doggsology for Three Voices' and 'The Old Story of the Widow and the Commercial Traveller' and involved scores of members in organising, writing, producing and performing.

For a long time the actual scripts avoided detection and it was thought that they had been burned in an effort to protect the blameworthy from humiliation, dishonour and personal abuse by future generations of members who may wish to extract the proverbial Michael. However, after a protracted and rigorous investigation a single script from the 1961 Revue has now been found, and remains a testament to the artistic creativity that once surged through the hearts and minds of Parklangley members.

The sketch is entitled 'Tried by the Centre Court' and was kindly provided by Mr Ron Swash who both wrote and performed the sketch.

Tried by the Centre Court

Set

One Umpire's Ladder One Score-book

Character

One Wimbledon Umpire

Scene

One man (the umpire) wearing a blue blazer and an old hat, sitting at the top of a short step-ladder or umpire's chair

Umpire

I'd like you to imagine that I'm wearing a blue blazer and an old hat, and that I'm sitting at the top of a short step-ladder. It's summer.

Wimbledon, June, Ladies singles, Third Round
Ball boys are bounding all over the ground
Play started at 2:00, and we're still on the rack
It's a quarter to five and they've hardly begun.
A solid defence meets a steady attack
Miss L. Hammerfest meets Miss J. Hunter-Dunn.
Game to Miss Hunter-Dunn
Miss Hammerfest leads by two games to one
In the third set, having won the first by 18 games to 16, and
lost the second by 25 games to 27.

Oh, I never liked Tennis.
Damned silly name for a game
with its volleys and loves and all that.
The first time I umpired was June 46.
I didn't think much of it then
(and I don't think much of it now).
I just fancied myself in the hat.
Since when I have umpired again and again and again.

And year after year as I've sat
On court after court
I've been struck by the thought
They are bashing a ball with the gut of a cat
What a sport!

You may think its tedious seen from down there.
Its ludicrous seen from above.

15 – love

Keeping my eye firmly fixed on the ball,
Hoping the linesman will know what to call

15 – all

As each long drawn out point
Puts my neck out of joint,
What a job!
Set after set. Oh the relief when you get an occasional lob!
A-a-a-a-a-ah! Till they smash it.
Ooh dash it.

30 – 15

What does it all mean?

40 – 15

Why 15–30, why 40–15, what if instead
I just said,
1–nothing, 2–nothing, 3–nothing and game.
It'd do just the same.
I suppose some of the older debenture holders 'ld be bound
to get shirty!

40 – 30

Now the spectators are trickling — 'Out'
There's thunder about
With luck it might rain; that ought to reduce
What the...

Deuce

Half of me bored.

Net-cord.

The other half nervous.
First service.
Wish it were time for dinner.
Thank God — A winner

Advantage Miss Hammerfest

Bonk. Bink. Bonk. Bink
Drives you to drink.

Sitting up here
I'm obsessed with the fear
Of getting it wrong —
that everyone else will be going bonk-bink
and I shall be going bink-bonk

Oh what is the use?
We're back again

Deuce

Groundsmen are asked: "How's the state of the ground?"
Players are photographed jumping the nets.
But here sits a figure one often forgets
The British Umpire, upon whom the sun never sets.

Mini Olympics

The Parklangley Club is split into 3 sections: Tennis, Squash and Badminton. Only a few brave souls ever attempt to join more than two of the three and, for those who do, it has been known to induce a mild emotional disorder brought on by split loyalties. In order to promote the natural feelings of competition that such a structure engenders, in the late 1970s the club started a yearly inter-section competition, known as the mini Olympics. Now, the rules were reasonably straightforward. Each section played the others at their own sport and whoever scored the most points at the end if the day could announce themselves on par with the Greek Gods and, more importantly, take ownership of bragging rights for the ensuing year.

In order to equalise the abilities of players from different disciplines, a simple rule was introduced. Team players of any sport could represent their section but could not play their own sport, in an attempt to ensure that a player with little or no experience of, for instance, badminton, did not have to play a team player from that section.

This seemed to work well for many years, generating much interaction between people who may not otherwise have had contact with each other. The records show that the Squash section usually won and when they didn't the Tennis section would reign triumphant. Now the Badminton section decided that this simply was not acceptable and, in what proved to be the final year of the mini-Olympics, picked Paul Whetnall, ex-British number one and British Olympic coach — that's the real Olympics, you know the one that happens every four years with the big opening ceremony — to play Badminton for the Badminton section. A quick look at the records revealed that Paul had not played for the teams and thus his inclusion as a Badminton player was within the rules, although about as far outside the spirit of the rules as it is possible to get.

As if to prove the old adage that cheats never prosper, the Badminton section, once again, came last.

Fêtes

Remember 1966 and all that? As well as England's famous World Cup victory, the year saw the first of a series of fêtes designed to raise money for the club as well as to have some fun. There were four in total in 1966, 1967, 1968 and 1970. The 1966 event was dubbed The Grand Fête and took place at Croydon Road Recreation Ground. It included a huge raffle with the first prize being a new Mini. The other three fêtes were held at the Parklangley Club with the 1967 one being opened by television presenter Peter Glaze.

PARK LANGLEY

Grand Fete

Sideshows include: Hoop-la, Bingo, Coconut Shy, Roll-a-Penny
Tombola, Card Darts, Treasure Hunt, etc.
Also many Stalls and Childrens Corner

★ **A TUG OF WAR TOURNAMENT** ★

DISPLAY BY THE

BECKENHAM DOG TRAINING SOCIETY

WIN-A-MINI COMPETITION

CROYDON ROAD RECREATION GROUND

SATURDAY 18th JUNE 1966

from 2.30 p.m. to 6.30 p.m. • Admission 6d., Children 3d.

All enquiries to Hon. Secretary, N. H. Liney, Esq., 186 Bromley Road,
Beckenham, Kent

ROYAL INSURANCE GROUP 27 LONDON ROAD, BROMLEY

Fig. 6.1 *Grand Fête, 1966*

Marquees

September 1986 saw the first of possibly the biggest social event ever to be held at Parklangley, when the Grand Marquee Weekend came to the club as part of the celebrations for its 75th Anniversay. Four more of these took place in 1997, 1999, 2001 and 2003. The effort put in by staff and members in support of such huge projects has been nothing short of phenomenal as, over the course of several days towards the end of the summer season, a veritable multitude of events was held. Apart from the main ball other events include discos, live bands, lunches, children's discos and quiz nights. The effort involved in staging such huge events, from the then small clubhouse with a kitchen that struggled to cope if more than 3 people turned up for dinner, was nothing short of spectacular. Many staff worked through the night taking just a short sleeping break as the club became their hotel for the duration of festivities.

Fig. 6.2 *Jenny and Dave Ash –
Marquee Ball*

In 2001 the event was held during the club rebuild, described elsewhere in this book, making the enterprise even more difficult than usual. Whilst preparing for 500 guests the day before the main ball, calamity came once more to Parklangley when a break in the main electricity cable feeding the club resulted in a total power blackout. Cometh the hour, cometh the cook. Instead of doing the sensible thing and cancelling the event, club membership was instantly galvanised and salmon strategically relocated to the kitchens of a small army of club members for cooking and storage under the guidance of club cook Sue Beddoe. The cable was repaired the next day and the ball, against the odds, went ahead as planned. It was generally agreed that the salmon was delicious. We were, by the way, lucky to have Sue Beddoe with us at all after she was locked and lost in a portable cooler at the previous marquee event in 1999! Thankfully she was found before hypothermia set in.

Chapter 7

The Changing Face of a Club House

It may be just another building but a clubhouse also represents the public face of a club to the world. It is the thing people take most notice of when they come to visit, and prospective members, be it consciously or subconsciously, leave wondering whether it would be a place in which they can happily sit and while away the hours. Architecturally it need not be fancy or groundbreaking; it needs neither majestic facades nor intricate cornices that display their beauty to the world. But rather it is a place that should be simple, homely and comfortable. It is a place where, for many members, the majority of their time will be spent, indulging in the necessary liquid refreshment, having tired out their limbs and exhausted their energies in dedication to their chosen sport. After the competition comes the reconciliation, when the arguments and disagreements on the court can be resolved in an atmosphere of congenial debate. When we can take time to reflect on that missed drop shot, to bask in the beauty of that stylish and sumptuous volley or, most likely, to bemoan the fact that despite all the toil and trouble we never seem to get any better.

This section, then, tells the story of where the stories are told; it is the story of a building, or rather of a series of buildings, in which so many have spent so much of their time. The Parklangley clubhouse as it is now is the third clubhouse to be built during the course of the last century, and the club boasts a number of members who have been around long enough to remember all three. The first two were far humbler buildings than the most recent manifestation but, nevertheless, had certain charms which are worth exploring. They contain a host of memories for club members and, to be fair, suffered from some ever so minor drawbacks.

Fig. 7.1 *The first Parklangley clubhouse, built 1911*

The first clubhouse was built in 1911. It has been speculated that the original owners had ambitious plans for an elegant and grandiose clubhouse but lacked the funds to fulfil their dream, in the end settling for the simple and practical building we see in the pictures here. Built with a minimum of fuss, on first impressions you could perhaps describe it as little more than a large hut, which seems at odds with the philosophy that the owners of the Parklangley estate were applying to the design and build of the surrounding area. Yet somehow the failure to create a grand architectural design helped to define what the club would become, for this lack of ostentation or pomposity has always suited the low key, easy going nature of the club's personality. I always judge a building by how I feel when I first look at it, and it seems to me this is just right in its simplicity.

The brick-built changing rooms, constructed in 1939, gave the clubhouse a more permanent feel.

The first clubhouse finally met its Waterloo after serving the club for 63 years, being demolished in 1974 and replaced by a building that, by today's standards at least, many would consider to be basic at best. The club did not offer a chef, a head cook or even a bottle washer but, along with a bar, the addition of a kitchen gave those who were so inclined the option to

Fig. 7.2 *Final days of the first Parklangley clubhouse, 1974*

prepare their own food. From the outside its flat roof and box-shaped exterior were aesthetically displeasing and, if memory serves me correctly, I have never heard anyone describe the building as beautiful. By 1987 three new badminton courts had been built and, by comparison, the clubhouse was beginning to look a little jaded. Someone visiting at this time might have come to the conclusion that the club, with its many tennis courts, squash courts and superb new badminton courts had excellent facilities, but that the clubhouse and changing facilities were, dare I say it, a bit of a dump.

Personally I would have had to disagree. From the outside, despite being aesthetically insignificant, architecturally pointless and, well, just a square box, the clubhouse did have character. By day its many windows flooded the interior with a soft light, and at night, despite its basic appearance, the low ceiling and soft lighting gave it a comfortable and relaxing atmosphere. Rather like your grandmother's living room when she hasn't tidied up for a few weeks, it somehow managed to meet the most important criteria for a good clubhouse — it was homely. And it had a further and, for some, a far more significant advantage, which is that the bar only closed when the last member left the building. It was rumoured the keys had been lost sometime soon after the clubhouse was built so it was often up to the last member standing to pull down the shutters, and I remember a time when

...on second thoughts best stop there through fear of falling foul of the licensing laws by incriminating the guilty.

Fig. 7.3 *The second Parklangley clubhouse, built 1974*

Times change of course and the plethora of new and generously funded clubs that abound in the Beckenham area were in danger of making the Parklangley clubhouse look like the metaphorical dinosaur. So, depending on your point of view, with either sadness and regret or happiness and relief the curtain was brought down on the second clubhouse in 2001 and replaced with the bright and shiny new building you can see today. The detailed story of the pain and anguish of this new development is told elsewhere in this book but, before 2002 was out the new building had risen from the vestiges of the old, to stand as a challenge to the modern new sports clubs that were being built to cater for the ever increasing wealth and demands of the British public.

So wood was replaced with brick, small was replaced with large, low ceiling was replaced with high ceiling and cheap was replaced with, er, not so cheap. If we are honest we have to say that the new clubhouse has had a mixed reception. It is of course much larger and imposes itself on the surrounding club grounds with far greater authority and presence. It is not aesthetically beautiful but neither is it ugly, and perhaps one would describe it as functional. Some members regret the passing of the old clubhouse and some simply cannot understand why they do. Perhaps it is because it held cherished memories, perhaps it's because the new building has a telly and the football is always on, but perhaps, in time, they might come to view the new clubhouse with the same affection as the old. Buildings need to be lived in.

One thing is for certain, there is no going back. The latest clubhouse was opened with great fanfare in 2002 by tennis champion Pat Cash. It is a building designed and constructed to compete in the modern leisure market and incorporates a larger bar, a modern kitchen, a studio, office space and meeting rooms, therapy suite, squash courts and a small gym, all under one roof. It is a building that seeks to ensure that the Parklangley Club has a future as well as a past and, given the prosperity the club has enjoyed since its completion, none can doubt the success of that ambition. Now, if only they could get the air conditioning to work in the men's changing rooms...

Fig. 7.4 *Then Chairman, Bill Diggens, opens the current clubhouse with Wimbledon champion Pat Cash*

Chapter 8

A Place Called Home – Parklangley in the Fifties and Sixties

"Be it ever so humble, there's no place like home", are the last lines of the 1822 John Payne song 'Home! Sweet Home!' lines with which we are all familiar, and which bring with them a feeling of security. This sense of security was about to arrive at the club as it entered its 5th decade.

In March 1940 the club had invested power in its members to manage the day to day activities. To The Parklangley Sports Club Limited, the members' club gave sufficient funds to pay the rent and other expenses, and the company entered into a new 21 year lease with the landlords, London and Kent Estates. This was due to expire in 1961 and, although there was an option to extend it for a further seven years, the terms meant that all premises and equipment would revert to the landlord when the lease expired.

It came to the committee's attention that London and Kent Estates were to go into liquidation and so, in what was arguably one of the most important moments in the club's history, the committee decided to see if they could obtain the freehold. Thus it came to pass that on the 14th of November 1952 ownership of the building passed to the club for the princely sum of £2,700 after fundraising efforts managed to achieve £4,100 made up as follows:

- 10 year loan for £1800, at 3% from the Lawn Tennis Association
- Donations from members £500
- 12 year debentures to members for £1800, at 4%

A new company, Parklangley Freeholds Ltd was formed to take ownership of the estate and to preserve its future as a sports ground, and the old Parklangley Sports Club Ltd was wound up. The generations of sportsmen and sportswomen of the surrounding area who have subsequently used the ground owe a debt of gratitude to those who showed the clarity and foresight, and expended no little effort, in ensuring the club remained under the ownership of its members with the stated aim of allowing members *"...to use the Club's premises in perpetuity"*.

Play in the Fifties and Sixties

In the November 2009 issue of the The Parklangley Club newsletter, tennis coach Mark Sheldon interviewed Wendy Nelson, a member who won the ladies singles title on a number of occasions in the 1950s. It is a charming interview and provides us with some alluring insights into the club at that time. The following is an extract from the interview:

> *I started playing tennis at the age of ten in 1940 in the midlands. My parents were both keen players. When we moved south I joined Parklangley in 1943. There was no coaching at the club but when I was 16 I had some Kent County coaching with a coach called Captain Rodgers! In 1948 I managed to win the U18 girls singles at Parklangley.*
>
> *It was a very friendly atmosphere and since I was a good player for my age adults were very happy for me to play with them.*

It was one of the only clubs in London that stayed open during the winter. And in fact it ran an Open Junior Tournament all through the war attracting many players who went on to be post-war names in the senior field. It was a great place to get to know people of all ages. I remember I knew a lot of adults by their first name which my parents found quite surprising. I remember knowing Donald Stotesbury then as 'Donald' and remember him pushing Michael Stotesbury around in a pram!

At that time the club had a small clubhouse, one badminton hall, ten grass courts and three hard courts. No floodlights, indoor courts or squash courts in those days! I was co-opted on to the committee as Junior Captain and went on to be match secretary, Ladies Captain and never got away from being a committee member!

I won five singles titles. I'm reminded of that when I come and see my grandchildren play and look up on the champions' board! I remember the Smith twins (including Pat who won in 1951). We always had highly competitive matches. It felt like a great achievement to win the Ladies singles in 1954 with them playing at the club. I played mixed doubles with John Best (men's singles winner on four occasions) which was a real privilege. He won the All England Mixed Doubles in the 50s and he also won the Badminton singles title at the club. We never won the mixed though we were runners up once. I won the badminton doubles in 1955 with Zena Urmston who I also partnered in tennis.

The interview tells us something of the club's major players during the period, for instance John Best, who was arguably Parklangley's most successful sporting export and other parts of this book contain details of his exploits. Pat and Pam Smith were, for many years, stalwarts of the tennis club, playing in a total of 28 finals between them, in all competitions, during the period 1946 to 1955. Being the father of twins I am personally sceptical as to whether there is some kind of telepathic and magical bond existing between them. However, it is reliably reported that they each bought their first houses in different areas, by co-incidence exchanging on the same day. Not until playing tennis later that same evening did they realise they had both purchased properties with a house number of 17. I leave you to judge. Zena Urmston was another significant player of the period and team captain for several years who also became a non-playing captain for Kent.

Fig. 8.1 *Finals day, 22nd July 1961 – Spectators left to right: Ann Kirch, David Crook, Willie Knoop, Doris Knoop (seated), H.C. Rowe, Eileen Stotesbury, Eileen Morrish, Mrs Rowe, Sheila Blake, Graham Nelson and* ⟨unknown⟩. *Players kneeling left to right: Bill Ford, Jennifer McIntosh, Stephanie Baldwin, Bert Pembro. Photographers left to right:* ⟨unknown⟩, *Wendy Nelson and Zena Urmston*

Given the size and number of courts at the club it is remarkable to think that it took until the 1950s for the Parklangley losing streak to be broken. In 1951–52 the Ladies 1st team won the winter Kent Cup division 2 and in 1958 the men's team won the summer Kent Cup at division 4. Having broken their duck the club pushed on and was even more successful in the sixties, winning a total of 15 Kent cups at various levels, including a mixed and two Ladies' victories in division 1, hardly surprising given the depth of women's talent available to the club at that time.

Fig. 8.2 *Donald Stotesbury presents a shield to John Cridland, Club Captain*

In the 50s lots of further development work, again much of it voluntary, was undertaken under the guidance of Grounds Chairman Donald Stotesbury. Three of the original courts were brought down to equal level, thereby creating room to add a fourth court. Subsequent grass courts, now numbering 11 in total, were adjusted to regulation length with ample runback.

Golden Jubilee

In 1961, the club's golden jubilee was celebrated with both a gala in the club grounds and a dinner dance at the Bromley Court Hotel. The dinner dance was attended by 160 members and a long standing past member, Mr Harold Dyer, toasted the club's achievements. At the gala the London Gymnastic Club provided an accomplished demonstration on parallel and horizontal bars, and a 'Memory Corner' of photographs and

other artefacts pertaining to the club's history was displayed. How strange
it seems to me that members of Parklangley were already looking back at
happy memories, successes and reminiscing on fifty years of history the
year after this author was born.

Reminiscing is all very well, of course, but those in charge of the club
always had an eye on the future and on ensuring the club's survival.
Consequently, a jubilee fund was started for club improvements. The
Jubilee Fete raised over £70. Many members gave considerable sums
including a donation of £15 from Mr. H. Olby — thought to have been
the largest single contributor. The jubilee fund was closed in April 1962
having raised the magnificent sum of £318 11s 10d.

If my aunt's memory serves her correctly this was almost enough to have
bought her first house in the late fifties. And lo and behold in 1961 the
club actually went and did just that, buying a house which is used as the
living quarters for the club grounds man, for £1,802. There were a number
of other fundraising events in the period including the revues (mentioned
above), 'guess the highest scores' weekly cricket competitions, and even
the purchase and retail of Parklangley pencils. The pencils were inscribed
'Parklangley L.T. & B. Club' and retailed for 6d (for those of you reading
this book who are under a certain age this equates to approximately two
and a half pence). The sellers obviously believed in the old adage that if
you look after the pennies the pounds will look after themselves, and this
is exactly what happened as the money raised aided the funding of one of
the most significant developments in the early sixties, namely the arrival
of floodlights for an outdoor court. 'Floodlights, for one court, a major
development?!', I hear you shout. To the modern member who has grown
up in a world where such facilities are commonplace I say, well, before
you decry such efforts, consider this: in the early sixties there were only
four tennis courts in the whole of London with such an advanced facility.

Showing the same ingenuity and self-reliance that had characterised their
fundraising activities, a few members, including Ron Swash, Ian Crane
and Peter Stotesbury, played on each of the existing floodlit courts to
assess the quality of light, position and type of lamp-poles, bulbs, lamp-
holders etc. They then gathered together enough Parklangley volunteers
to dig the trenches, lay the cable and erect the poles at a total cost of

just over £400. The result was considered to be the best outdoor floodlit court in the whole country and was officially opened with an exhibition match featuring Geoff Paish, Pauline Roberts and Jill and Alan Mills (who, incidentally, went on to become tournament referee at Wimbledon from 1982 to 2005).

Continuous Improvement

Despite the sterling efforts of members towards the end of the sixties, the club facilities were looking a little shoddy. The original clubhouse and changing rooms were in a state of disrepair and many considered the amenities ever so slightly substandard. Once again the club responded and in 1965 formed a development committee with the aim of improving club facilities.

The development proved to be a protracted affair, with the initial phase shifting and morphing between ideas as conflicting priorities shaped progress. The first idea was to replace the clubhouse and old badminton hall but, as time went by, new changing rooms and the addition of squash courts came into contention. If we consider 1965 as the beginning of the project, and 1974 — when the second of Parklangley's clubhouses was finally rebuilt — the end, it lasted fully 9 years. By the same criteria the channel tunnel took over 300 years, so Parklangley Development Committees are not as slow as you might think.

The money was to be raised by large-scale raffles, fetes, donations, and loans. No effort was to be spared to gather the necessary capital. An early innovative attempt, aimed at Parklangley residents who were not members, was a leaflet dispatched locally requesting that 'As this scheme will increase the amenities of the neighbourhood, especially for the future generation, all local residents are asked to support the effort'. There is no information recording the success of this initiative but it's worth noting the appeal on behalf of future generations.

Notwithstanding local apathy the club decided to embark on a series of fetes which took place in 1966, '67, '68 and '70. The one in 1966, which was dubbed The Grand Fete, took place at Croydon Road Recreation Ground, and included a huge raffle. The first prize, a new Mini, was won by Terry Johnson and presented by local MP John Hunt. The other three fetes were held at the Parklangley Club, and the 1967 fete was opened by television presenter Peter Glaze. If you do not remember him just cast your mind back (if you are old enough of course) to the immortal catch phrase, 'It's Friday, it's five o'clock, it's Crackerjack!'.

Here's another brief aside: In Crackerjack sketches, Peter Glaze was often cast as a pompous twit, who would get exasperated with his comedy partner Don Maclean during the course of a sketch. Maclean would then give an alliterative retort, such as "Don't get your knickers in a knot" or "Don't get your tights in a twist", the combination of which — 'Don't get your knickers in a twist' — has long since passed into the popular vernacular. Anyway, back to business. The official programme from the 1967 fete provides insight into the thinking and priorities at the early stages of development:

> ...the present Pavilion is in a very bad condition and all members agree that rebuilding and replacement is essential, both to attract new members and to preserve the open space amenities of a sports club. In order to put a building scheme into operation we must raise an initial £7,000. We will, of course, be able to obtain part of this sum through loans, but the Club cannot afford to be too heavily committed in this way.

But the programme notes of the subsequent fete in 1968 show some new thinking:

> During the time since we started this scheme we have been constantly watching current trends. One of these is the increasing popularity of squash and we have decided that it would be in the best interests of both the Club and the district for us to include this in our plans... It is then hoped that at a later date that we will be able to build a new Badminton Hall.

And with that statement it was clear that the club was about to get its third sport.

Chapter 9

Into the Seventies

The Squash Man Cometh

Some sports historians — but not all as historians never actually agree on anything — will inform you that the game of squash originated in the 19th century at Harrow School, and was derived from the game of Racquets, and that the first recorded construction of purpose-built squash courts was at Harrow in the 1860s. It is possible that earlier squash courts were created at Harrow by sub-dividing a racquets court, which is almost exactly the size of three Squash courts (to allow more players on the courts at the same time). The game generally remained the preserve of schools and universities until the early part of the 20th century, by which time it was becoming popular in the private clubs such as the RAC in London.

The sport slowly gained in popularity until the 1970s and 1980s, which witnessed a massive jump in participation, and a staggering rise in the number of new clubs and courts. This squash boom infiltrated its way into popular culture and squash was often characterised as an upmarket game for aspiring young macho businessmen. In the movie Wall Street its main protagonists, Michael Gekko and Charlie Bud, vie for supremacy on the squash court, an enduring symbol of a hard-nosed, competitive and ruthless business environment.

Fig. 9.1 *Graham Jordon, six times squash open champion, with world champion Chris Dittmar*

But at Parklangley things were a little different. By the late 1960s the club had seen a decline in income from tennis, and again faced serious financial difficulties. As we have seen, some money had been raised by a series of revues and other events in the preceding years and, once again, the club's knack of finding the right people to make the decisions at the right time came to the fore. Donald Stotesbury in particular was instrumental in persuading the club to invest in new squash courts, at the expense of a new clubhouse, displaying a shrewd awareness of the booming interest in squash at the start of the seventies. Thus two new squash courts were built in 1971 with Peter Stotesbury, Donald's son, becoming the first chairman of the squash section which existed as a division of the tennis section until a new constitution was established in 1974. Membership of the squash section was fully taken up before the new courts were completed and the early squash years were dominated by Dave Manning who won the squash championship from 1975 to 1979, a string of five consecutive victories only equalled by Graham Jordon whose five year reign started in 1986.

To take into account the dawning of a new sport at the club, further re-organisation saw it become The Parklangley Club, a name that it has kept to this day, although it was not until 1974 that a new constitution was finally completed. While this new constitution was 'under construction' the club, between 1970 and 1974, was managed by an erstwhile Gang of Four affectionately nicknamed the PIGs (Provisional Interim Government) who consisted of chairman Alan Whitehead, Ian Crane, Dennis Reeley and Peter Stotesbury.

It is hard to believe that by the early 1990s the boom sport had almost gone bust, with the Squash Rackets Association in a state of disarray as it relinquished organization of many of its major events. A cursory look at the huge building programme of courts may help to explain why. In the three years to March 1984 there was an 8% increase in participation but this was met by a 25% increase in the number of courts. Many squash clubs had been set up to offer only the single sport and either closed down or turned themselves into multi sports venues with squash taking a minor role.

Parklangley, as so often, managed to buck the trend and added further courts, one in 1991 and a further in 2001, which was part of the new club development discussed elsewhere in this book. Furthermore both courts were opened by two former world number ones and greats of the modern era, the 1991 court being graced by the sublime talents of Australian Chris Dittmar and the 2001 court by the solid Scot Peter Nichol. At the risk of being accused of inserting some self promotion into these pages I'll add that, being a reasonable standard club member, I had the honour of playing against both players at these exhibition matches. Erstwhile UK squash coach, events organizer and referee at both matches, Neil Harvey, asked me after the second who was the better player. Having been held to a single point by both (well, they needed to keep the crowd involved somehow so perhaps I should re-phrase that to say 'having been permitted a single point by both') I had to reply that it was a rather impossible question to answer.

Anyway, enough of my personal reminiscences. The squash was an excellent addition to the Parklangley Club and once again it had found members with the foresight and willingness to get involved, and to raise and commit the necessary funding. Their faith was repaid as membership grew and the finances improved, especially, as all good squash members will know, those finances associated with bar takings.

Pressures for Change

But, of course, everything changes. In the sixties, seventies and eighties things seemed to be changing faster than ever. Despite the headline news of industrial unrest, strikes and oil crises, in the decades since the sixties the western world was getting richer. New sports clubs were appearing all over the country with the financial backing of huge organisations who could afford the capital investment required for the very best facilities. People's expectations of the type of facilities they could enjoy with their increased wealth were rising. At Parklangley things remained steady. New kitchens were built in 1971, the clubhouse was rebuilt in 1974, in 1977 three tennis courts were converted to all weather surfaces with additional floodlights added in 1979 and 1981.

In the tennis arena the club continued to compete in regular inter-Kent matches and the 1970s was dominated by a young Nick Evans who won the men's singles title every year from 1971 to 1977. Nick was feted as a potential English star after beating Australian Ken Rosewall in a friendly match in his early teens and whisked off to Bisham Abbey for intensive training with the LTA. Unfortunately he failed to make further significant headway.

In an effort to be more efficient the nature of the club's management structure underwent significant changes during this period. For some time all three sections ran their own affairs as separate entities. In May 1974 all three sections were amalgamated, and the running of the club was centralised under a new management committee. By 1979 the club's finances were also centralised as each of the sections no longer had separate accounts. John Norton was appointed as club treasurer and is thought to be the first paid administrative club employee.

Despite these responses to a fast moving sports market the club was soon facing its next financial problems. It was not so much that the club was going backwards, more that it was being left behind by the progress of its competitors. In the early '80s income was generally about £25,000 a year with a surplus of just £2,000. Membership was falling; there was no reception or anybody else available to whom prospective members could talk. Facilities were falling into disrepair and the changing rooms, if subject to a present day health and safety inspection, would have been closed down. The temporary badminton hall — yes, remember the one built in 1912 with a 2 year licence — remained the focal point of the club, being utilised for badminton, quiz nights, discos and parties many of which had to be abandoned if it rained too heavily. Many clubs with similar constitutions to Parklangley, such as Cyphers, were in a similar situation and regrettably closed down.

Membership was low and starting to fall — in the mid 80s the combined adult membership for all sports stood at a paltry 400. Once again the Parklangley Club stared into the abyss, didn't like what it saw, and decided to do something about it.

Chapter 10

The Age of Professionalism

In history there are often pivotal moments, key decisions or choices that change and alter for ever the direction of events. For the Parklangley Club the Annual General Meeting of 1984 was such a moment, as it started a chain of events that fundamentally changed the nature of the club; when the ethos of unpaid part time management began the long march towards professionalism.

Alan Whitehead had been chairman of the Club from the formation of the new structure in 1974. He felt that he was lacking new ideas, but could not find anyone willing to replace him, so at the 1984 AGM he forced the issue: he did not stand for re-election, but instead accepted the role of Financial Executive from Dennis Howells who retired owing to ill health. This meant that the Management Committee left the AGM without a Chairman.

At the first meeting of the new Management Committee on 12th December 1984, at which Alan Whitehead was deliberately absent, Tony Beddoe was persuaded by Roy Kelly and others to take on the chairmanship provided that the committee would look favourably on the idea of employing a full time Club Manager. Consequently, in the autumn of 1985 Stephen Holmes was appointed the first Club Manager

This was the real and lasting change that sprang from the 1984 meeting because it revolutionised the way the Club was run. The idea of the chairman of the time performing day to day administration ably abetted by a management committee that slowly, if surely, raised funds to facilitate minor improvements was dead. Seen through the prism of the current clubhouse and its 70 plus paid employees, it's difficult to fully appreciate the scale of this change but it was probably the most revolutionary moment in the club's history. Now we are not quite talking the storming of the Bastille or the power grab of the Bolsheviks in 1914 but, nonetheless, the old Parklangley way of doing things, established over the preceding 75 years, was no more. The new approach included an autonomous and proactive manager, and targets for subscriptions, income and coaching. When the club needed to change in order to adapt to the prevailing requirements, it once again found the impetus to do so. The table below details the significant increase in income generated by the new approach, largely due to the hiring of professionally paid club management.

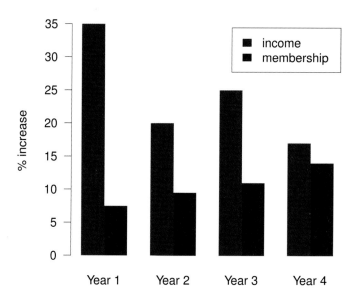

Fig. 10.1 *Bar chart showing increase in income and membership following the initiation of a new approach*

Despite the new professionalism, the building of the new Badminton hall remained reassuringly Parklangleyish (did I just invent a new word?). The two builders employed to erect the new Badminton courts lived on site, and it is reported that they were not seen for several weeks at a time, during which cans of lager would stack up outside their caravan. The site was completed the day before the infamous hurricane which swept through the United Kingdom in October 1987. It occurred during one of the contractors' rare trips to the office, and they returned to find a chestnut tree had been uprooted and landed within a foot of their caravan. They responded to this moment of adversity in typical style, using the tree to prop up subsequent cases of lager.

The snowball of professionalism gathered pace. In 1990, after the first paid club manager, Stephen Holmes left, his successor, Tony Beddoe, was appointed. Tony had been the club chairman at the time of the 'revolution' and pushed forward the modernising agenda with vigour. By September 1st 1990 two new indoor tennis courts were in place. Needless to say the usual nightmares of gaining planning consent, finding the finances and project build were experienced to the full. The project cost £230,000 but the outlay proved a good investment as membership figures soared. Holding all out professionalism at bay, erstwhile club manager Stephen Holmes completed all the light fittings — an arrangement everyone was happy with on the basis that he appeared to know what he was doing. The courts were opened by Mark Cox and were immediately popular with members, providing an instant and much welcomed increase in cash flow.

Two further projects were completed in 1991. Firstly the club goat was unceremoniously removed from its feeding patch at the rear of what is now the car park furthest from the clubhouse, along with the 400 cubic metres of rubble that had built up over the years, and was replaced with a new outdoor tennis court. The goat had been the idea of then groundsman Glen Morgan as a novel form of labour saving and was used to help keep the grass courts under control. However, times were a changing and, after escaping and eating significant amounts of vegetation from surrounding gardens, it was generally agreed that the goat had to go. Secondly the car park was extended to encompass the two parking areas furthest from the club house. This brought problems of its own as the increased tarmac and reduced drainage area resulted in what was to become know as the phenomenon of the Parklangley Lake — the huge expanse of water that built up in the driveway adjacent to the two far parking areas. After multiple attempts to deal with the issue the lake was drained for the last time after the building of additional drainage facilities in 2008.

Further advancement saw the building of a new squash court in 1991. Again money was tight but the club was nothing if not creative in its efforts to raise money, offering loans to members, life memberships and the 'buy a brick' initiative. This gave members the opportunity to have their names engraved and immortalised on one of the bricks used in the new build for the princely sum of £50. It is a matter of historical record that a number of members took up this offer — it is rumoured that one day soon the engraving will commence. The formal opening of the new court was a superb occasion as the club was honoured with an exhibition match featuring Chris Dittmar, world number one.

In 1993, three tarmac courts were resurfaced to floodlit artificial grass and, in 1994, two more tarmac courts became acrylic. So by the turn of the millennium the club had 16 tennis courts — 2 indoor, 8 grass, 2 floodlit acrylic, 3 floodlit artificial grass and 1 tarmac — a modern, specially-designed 3 court badminton hall and 3 squash courts (the new one had facilities to seat over a hundred people for exhibition matches).

The temporary 1911 badminton hall was still alive and well having managed to survive not only the best part of a century, but also a fire in the mid 1990s. Because of its ageing appearance it had been decided that it would benefit from a quick facelift. During the redecoration the wall heaters were placed on top of a temporary room that had been built on the stage at the front, and which was used as a treatment room for a new physiotherapist who had recently joined the club. Whoever moved the radiators had neglected to turn them off and over time the heat built up until a fire started. Luckily, if one can consider a fire lucky, it started during one of the hall's many dance nights and was noticed by Stan Wilson who proceeded to engage in a number of chicken runs from the bar to the hall with containers of water. Stan's efforts were, thankfully, successful in damping the flames. One assumes this occurred before the health and safety culture had so totally captured our consciousness, as most members reportedly sat dispassionately, continuing their consumption of intoxicating liquids, as they scrutinised Stan's gallant efforts. So raise a glass to Stan, as without his heroics and presence of mind we would probably now have 'no club.

Fig. 10.2 *A Young Mark Sheldon collects one of his many club titles*

In men's tennis the late '80s and early '90s were dominated by Mark Sheldon who won the first of his 9 titles in 1987. Mark, along with Kestor Jackson, went on to play collegiate tennis in America. On their return both continued their long standing relationship with the club as coaches and Mark proved his dexterity by also winning both the men's squash and racquetball tournaments and tying English international Colin 'Beech Boy' Beecher to the club goat, an experience from which the goat never recovered.

Bits and Bytes

It seems such a long time ago, 1999, but there was a particular unease in the air. The so-called Y2k problem, the inability of computers to read dates beyond 1999, threatened to turn January 1st, 2000 into a nightmare. The issue had first been noticed by programmers in the 1950s, but had been ignored. As the turn of the century loomed, it seemed that humankind faced disaster.

Aircraft would fall from the skies; electricity grids, water systems and telephone networks would be knocked out, while nuclear power plants would go into meltdown, and savings and pension accounts would be wiped out in a general bank failure. The Y2k catastrophe was promoted with increasing shrillness toward the century's end: headlines proclaimed a *"computer time bomb"* or *"a date with disaster as governments and corporations set in place immensely expensive schemes to immunize systems against the Y2k bug."* The Italians, by the way, did nothing.

But let's not forget what was probably the most important problem of all facing club members, namely that the Parklangley computer system would fail, meaning members would be unable to book courts. The initial computer revolution may have passed Parklangley by — but then that's true of virtually every sports club of its size — but by the year 2000 few could match Parklangley's range of functions that had been, and continue to be, computerised. These include a database of all membership details, subscriptions, direct debit for membership fees and court bookings, accounts, an internet based booking system, management of coaching programmes and even lighting control.

Anyway, as the 2000 doomsday came and went, with minor glitches that would have gone unnoticed any other day of the week, the world kept ticking on. It must have been irritating for computer-conscientious Germans — who had spent a fortune remedying a non existent problem — to observe how life continued its pleasurable path for feckless Italians, and for the Parklangley Club which also, as I understand it, did nothing.

As with all computer systems the Parklangley system has its detractors and the vagaries of the user interface for members can be ever so slightly impenetrable for the technophobes among us. However I would be willing to wager that no club of comparative size, indeed even the corporate giants who manage multiple clubs, have anything so extensive and useful. For an undertaking the size of Parklangley one should not underestimate the impact of this system in terms of reducing its cost base and helping to provide an advantage in an increasingly competitive marketplace. From my own admittedly unscientific estimates, after a number of sojourns into the chaos that constitutes the Parklangley office, I would hazard to guess that it negates the need for 3 to 4 full time staff. Now, if only we could get it to answer the phone before we have to wait 27 rings. On second thoughts that would mean yet another menu of automated phone options as long as your arm — lets keep the 27 rings service — as everyone knows, it takes a while to pour a pint of Guinness before the bar staff have time to make it to the phone.

Children – The Rise and Rise

Over the last thirty years few of us have failed to notice the profound changes in the way we now bring up children, with child-centered, controlled activities replacing the more time-honoured pastime of kids kicking a ball about in the street. In the past the darling offspring of club members were once of little significance, existing here and there in small, dark corners of the club, seen but seldom heard. A far cry from what we see today, as endless millions of sweet little things daily swarm through the club like a plague of locusts, consuming more chips and chicken nuggets than seems good for them. This change has been nothing short of revolutionary and is a social phenomenon which extends far beyond the borders of Parklangley.

It is a change that has generated much controversy and bar debate at the club, between those who see it as a great opportunity for children to have fun, the breeding ground for an army of future members and a cash flow to die for, and those who believe it is a direct infringement of their civil liberties. If one single person can be given the credit for bringing about this revolution then that is the redoubtable ex-teacher Pam Robson, the club's third longest serving full time employee next to groundsman Mick Proffitt and current manager Tony Beddoe. I have to refrain from opinion on this subject as this author has another role as the husband of said Mrs Robson, and thus prudence prevents me from pronouncing further, albeit to say it is a debate that still has much traction and will generate heat for some time to come; probably forever, in fact.

It began in the late 1990s when Pam decided to start a gymnastics programme in the 'old badminton hall'. (Yes, the same badminton hall with the two year licence built in 1911. I cannot recall the number of activities the hall has been used for but if anyone should feel inclined to count them then please let me know). Anyway, hundreds of children turned up. They were soon offered mini tennis, which also boomed, and sometime later holiday programmes affording a full range of activities appeared, to entertain, amuse and improve our little darlings during those times of the year when teachers disappear from the planet. And then, just as you thought it was safe to return to the tennis courts, the parties. Oh yes, the parties. First a trickle, then a storm and then a veritable flood.

Such has been the success of children's ventures that, in its first Ofsted inspection, the club was graded as outstanding in several areas and achieved the highest Ofsted report in Kent. I have no real idea of the number of children who now use the club but some weekends up to nine children's parties are booked, and junior tennis and mini tennis coaching regularly involves almost 2000 children. These are highly impressive numbers. How much cash they bring to the club when one considers the booking fees, coaching fees and bar revenues generated by the parents and guardians is a matter of much speculation, but you can be sure that the kids are here to stay.

The changes that swept through the club in the 1980s and '90s were revolutionary enough, in Parklangley terms at least, but with the benefit of hindsight we could perhaps see them as the harbinger of what was to become the largest single project the Parklangley Club has undertaken since inception. The clubhouse and the facilities you can see around you now is the result of decades of dreaming, planning, heartache and hard-work of a small army of people. It involves numerous difficulties and setbacks but ultimately is the story of the triumph of a poorly funded members club to take control of its own destiny. This is the story told in the next chapter.

Chapter 11

A New Home

To understand the story of the genesis of the new club house we need to go back to the late 1980's and observe the confluence of some otherwise unrelated but nevertheless crucial events. The modernising agenda was fully under way and two decisions in particular, it seems to me, were the catalysts for the club to find the courage and breathing space for thinking bigger than the Parklangley consciousness had ever thought before. One of these came from a good idea and one was born of bad experience. First the bad experience. In the late 1980's the club's tennis coaching programme was set up very differently from how it is run today. The need to protect the guilty and steer clear of libel forbids me from naming individuals but at that time the head tennis coach, said to have been very charming and charismatic, also controlled the finances of the coaching programme. He took the money for coaching and paid the coaches himself. Except one day he didn't. Pay them that is, not take the money. Then, like a magician's assistant, he disappeared — only in this case there was no puff of smoke and he was never seen again. Some say he retired to a life of luxury in the Bahamas, others that he opened up a fish and chip shop in Scunthorpe. All we know for certain is that he left in his wake furious club management, accusations, recriminations and, most importantly, poor tennis coaches — many of whom were self employed and never saw any of their missing earnings.

He also set up a tournament involving the visit of a group of Norwegian juniors and neglected to tell anyone about it. When their organiser rang to confirm timings for arrival the tennis committee transformed into a group of headless chickens. But it is the nature of Parklangley to turn adversity to its advantage and by the end of the day lodgings for all visiting juniors had been found, and a tournament organised along with a wonderful spread for our Scandinavian visitors who were overwhelmed by the superb manner in which their visit and tournament had been organised.

Anyway, the law of unintended consequences being what it is, from the depths of adversity sprang hope. Administration of the tennis programme was brought 'in house' and a new coaching programme set up with Michelle Wheeler employed as the first full time coaching administrator. This became so successful that Parklangley soon found itself managing coaching programmes across a number of locations. Success followed success, short tennis for children was introduced by Sandi Proctor and, before you knew it there were hundreds, indeed thousands of people of all ages receiving coaching and, importantly, making use of the clubhouse and other facilities.

The second decision of import was rather more planned. In 1989 in an effort to extend the use of the facilities, it was decided to establish a daytime programme of activities directed at mothers with young children. This called for the creation of a crèche, a truly revolutionary idea in Parklangley terms. Sue Wilson was tasked with the unenviable job of starting it and running it in a club house that some said was not fit for the hordes of cockroaches that had made it their home, let alone an array of babies and young children. The pest controllers must have done a good job for soon the activities mornings were buzzing and many more people were using the sporting facilities and the club house.

I'm not suggesting a crèche and an unscrupulous tennis coach were the only significant factors that led to the development of a multi million pound sporting facility, but the use of club facilities was now at unprecedented levels. However, in their wake, came a problem of success: so many people were availing themselves of the facilities that it became apparent that there were more people using the ageing clubhouse than the ageing clubhouse could comfortably accommodate. By the mid-nineties significant additional funds had been spent on its upkeep despite the fact that it had obviously outlived its usefulness. A new clubhouse was much needed.

In the early to mid nineties several draft plans for redevelopment were drawn up by the club, with Mick Roberts, Mike Kelly and Tony Beddoe driving the agenda, but all seemed to flounder for a multitude of reasons. A development committee was established in 1997 at the behest of chairman Bill Diggens and, after several months of design work a design was approved at that year's AGM.

Approving it at the AGM was, of course, only the first milestone. There followed the two great battles that effectively turned the club into what you can see today — namely the battle for planning permission and the fight for funding.

In terms of funding, the two most important sources were the National Lottery and the Lawn Tennis Association. Bill Diggens bravely tackled the bureaucratic nightmare that was the funding application process for the National Lottery, which included a funding request form that contained no less than 70 appendices, only to be knocked back when the request for funding was rejected on two grounds. First, by investing in its sports facilities, the club had already seen a massive increase in participation to the point where facilities were largely booked out, and key questions on the lottery questionnaire require answers to how future participation would increase with lottery funding. Secondly, and potentially more intractably, Beckenham was considered too wealthy an area to be worthy of lottery funding.

If the club was to realise its dream, more lottery money was essential. A meeting was arranged at which club manager, Tony Beddoe, delivered a presentation to the National Lottery and explained to them the 'flawed and illogical nature' of their thinking, in his own unique and inimitable manner. Unbelievers expected that Tony's message would fall on deaf ears but his powers of persuasion being what they are the National Lottery, to their credit, both listened to and accepted his arguments: that having invested to increase participation the club needed more money to sustain it, and that an increase in participation in Bromley was surely no less deserving of funding than an increase of participation in Hackney. Consequently the National Lottery initially awarded The Parklangley Club the generous sum of £450,000.

Fig. 11.1 *Tony Beddoe by Tony Tidy*

Further persistence aligned to the club's excellent reputation with the LTA also paid dividends when they awarded the club £750,000 — which was made up of a £300,000 grant and a £450,000 loan. A further £100,000 loan from the brewery, a bank loan of £500,000 and surplus club funds raised total project capital to £2.3 million. Filled with optimism and hope, the club set a maximum budget of £2.5 million.

Having presented plans to the builders, the initial estimate came in at £2.9million. Consequently the plans had to be cut significantly with much of the upper floor, including the studio, sacrificed on the altar of financial expediency. Additionally the National Lottery's risk adversity meant that their funding would only be available after the build was well under way. Nevertheless the dye was cast and so, with a leap of faith, the largest and most expensive project the Parklangley Club has ever undertaken commenced. Remarkably, the majority of facilities were kept open for the duration of the build and staff worked in very difficult conditions in what became known as 'Portakabin City'.

Further funding efforts by members and additional lottery promises meant that something close to the original plans became possible. Nevertheless costs started to escalate at an uncontrollable rate. After all, this was a building project. For instance, the first building to be erected was the new Badminton Hall but shortly after its completion disaster struck. For obvious reasons the party responsible cannot be named here but within the week the new floor had been destroyed by damp as the walls had not been waterproofed. Badminton moved to indoor tennis while the walls were rebuilt.

As regards the main building and facilities the site survey proved to have little bearing on what was actually found when, shortly after work began, the foundations collapsed in on themselves. Metal spikes had to be inserted into the ground to strengthen the foundations causing a 6 to 8 week delay with significant knock on effects in terms of time and cost. Just to prove the old adage that bad things come in threes, at about the same time the club lost a battle with the VAT man to the tune of £350,000.

Despite these setbacks the Parklangley spirit somehow managed to prevail and the club house and new facilities were completed at a cost of £3.8 million, paid for as follows:

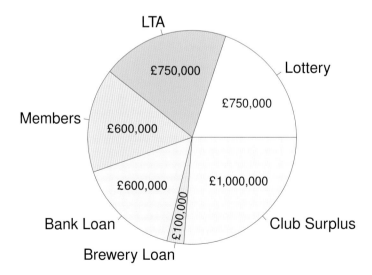

Fig. 11.2 *Pie chart of funding for the new facilities*

A few teething problems

Well, more than a few actually. The showers now required more water than the water supply could manage and the air conditioning rarely worked resulting in an out of court settlement with the electrical engineers. I could wax lyrical and make this book longer than anyone would wish it to be so let's just say it took all of 5 years to deal with the glitches. The build left the club with debts of £1.85 million which, at the time of writing, now stands at approximately £1 million. The club's intention is to pay off this debt within the next 10 years, leaving in place a thriving club ready to face the challenges and competition of the future.

The Success of Coaching and the Rise of a Superpower

As we have seen, the vastly improved facilities, the efficiencies of the computer system and a concentration of child activities and coaching have enabled the club to grow and prosper. To complete the picture we really need to understand a bit more about the impact that the unprecedented growth in tennis coaching has had on the club. Arguably the single biggest factor driving the success was the growth of short tennis under the management of Sandi Proctor, as thousand of children and their parents attended the club. Many were converted to full members thus feeding into the main tennis programmes. So many people were signing on for it that it became almost impossible to manage without the appointment of a Director of Coaching. This rise in coaching was underpinned by a number of other initiatives that coalesced into a virtual cycle of ever increasing activity, revenue and profit, with a cradle-to-grave strategy that included parent and child tournaments, the Summer Junior club, a children's holiday programme, a crèche, the Fred Harbour tournament, the Davis Cup, and ladies groups offering squash, badminton, racketball and tennis coaching.

As the activities grew it became apparent that there was insufficient space available to accommodate everybody. There was no more land at the club on which to build new facilities so there was really only one solution — world domination. Before long the energy, approach and coaching model pioneered at Parklangley spread as various sites were taken over and managed by the club, including Beckenham Recreation Ground, Kelsey Park, Willett Way, Old Dunstonians and Wickham Park. The latter was a separate club consisting of about 40 members but, as a sign of the Parklangley Club's maturing management approach and capability, this number soon stood at 250.

The table below shows the number of groups being coached by the mid nineties on site at Parklangley and off site at the various locations the club now managed.

Coaching Group	Groups on site	Numbers on site	Groups off site	Numbers off site
Short Tennis	32	350	7	110
Junior Tennis	65	360	83	482
Adult Tennis	17	140	12	90
Junior Badminton	7	70	–	–
Junior Squash	6	50	–	–
Special Needs	4	35	–	–
Totals	131	1005	102	682

According to LTA estimates it takes 10,000 hours of coaching over a period of 10 years to baseline a young player for entry into the rigours of the modern professional game. Parklangley has taken this philosophy to heart and its 'kids to adults' approach has started to bear fruit producing several successful players now ranked at County and National level. The club has developed into a 'Higher Satellite Centre' under the guidance of coaching directors Chris Merrick and Harry Bushnell, whose job is to prepare players for entry into the LTA High Performance Centres. At the time of writing, five players in the men's Kent County rankings started their careers at the club, including Kent number 1 Sean Thornley. Women are also doing rather well, with the club coaching programme boasting two of the top three Kent players in Emily Redbourne, and Naomi Cavaday who has now appeared at Wimbledon twice and is ranked number 5 in the UK.

It is a fact universally acknowledged that a club in possession of so many talented youngsters should be doing rather well in their local inter club leagues. However, the truth of this observation appears to have passed Parklangley by. This is partly because it sends its protégées off to the LTA Higher Performance Centres but also because part of its central ethos, as a members club, is to ensure its members remain focal to its ambitions. Thus, unlike many other clubs, it rarely pays top level players for their services.

Intra club competition for all sports, as ever, continues to be fierce with J. Barnett and Zoe Twidle dominating men's and women's tennis in recent years, and squash titles have taken on a dynastic flavour with the father and son duo of Clive and Steve London winning 8 of the last 12 singles titles.

That just about brings the story of the Parklangley Club up to date. As I feel duty-bound to mention once more, there will have been many people across the last century who have made a positive impact or contribution to the club and who do not feature within this book. Some, I'm sure, whom I have not even come across during my investigations. Although they may be absent from its pages, I hope they see this work as a fitting tribute to their efforts. One thing I have discovered is that a century is a very long time in the history of a sports club like Parklangley.

Chapter 12

The Next 100 Years

And so there it is. From its humble beginnings the Parklangley Club has grown to become, arguably, the premier all round rackets club of South East England. Despite stiff competition from its corporate competitors it continues to win awards, including LTA UK Club of the Year 3 times, Club of the Year for the South East and Club of the Year in Kent 2008. Within the Kent area it can lay claim to be a leader in a significant number of areas including the first club to implement Internet court bookings; computerised lighting; more people on coaching programmes than any other club; the only club with international competition level badminton courts; and, additionally, Parklangley has created an income stream which is the envy of its competitors.

It is unusual for a not-for-profit members club to reach these exalted heights. Such a level of success bears testament not only to the fact that there's really nothing on the telly anymore, but also to the hard work of its employees, the club's super-strong ethos of participation and its civic spirited culture. Despite now providing a living for over 70 paid employees, many of whom now actually do some work, the club continues to foster this culture, promoting sporting participation for people of all ages and abilities.

The last 100 years has seen massive social and political change, to which many similar but less well motivated clubs failed to adapt, lacking either the vision or energy to renew themselves at crucial times. Yet the Parklangley Club has survived this evolving world, thanks to those who gave of their time, effort and expertise. With a constitution that now enshrines its status in law as a community amateur sports club, its modern facilities and a reliable financial position, the future of the club seems assured.

If I were to take the liberty of speculating on what the next one hundred years might bring I would make the following predictions:

- The club will still exist

- The club will have produced a Wimbledon champion (far fetched, I know)

- Fifty years from now a new clubhouse will have been built

- In the new clubhouse the air conditioning in the men's toilets still won't work and a method of reliably and effectively cleaning them will remain beyond the reach of club management; a firm of consultants from Bangalore will be brought in and will troubleshoot the problem in three days, charging peanuts for their services.

Most importantly, though, I hope the club will continue to attract members willing to do something, however large or small, to contribute to its wellbeing, building on the success and legacy of the illustrious predecessors who have so colourfully peopled the pages of this book. These past generations parade through the clubs grounds unheard and unseen, and yet the ghostly authority of those who set things in motion, but have disappeared from the scene, continues to guide its future. I am reminded of the wish that the early member hoped for after the inaugural club championship *"Well, here endeth the first Tennis Club Entertainment, but I jolly well hope it won't be the last"*, a sentiment I can only echo one hundred years later. Indeed, my fondest wish is that, perhaps a hundred years from now, when I myself am but a minor footnote in the great ongoing saga of Parklangley, someone will find an aging copy of this book lost on an old Kindle in a dusty loft — if people still have dusty lofts — and decide to write a sequel. I wish him or her all the very best of British luck with it.

Appendix A

Men's Singles Tennis Champions 1911–2010

1914	R H HURLBAT	1953	L J CRIDLAND	1982	A J RICHARDSON
1919	R W INGRAM	1954	L J CRIDLAND	1983	A J RICHARDSON
1920	R W INGRAM	1955	J R BEST	1984	K JACKSON
1921	C WICKERS	1956	J R BEST	1985	K JACKSON
1922	E A KENDALL	1957	C M O'BRIEN	1986	E A THOMPSON
1923	E A KENDALL	1958	R P C SWASH	1987	M SHELDON
1924	E A KENDALL	1959	W H FOORD	1988	M SHELDON
1925	J DELOFORD	1960	B P PEMBRO	1989	M SHELDON
1926	J DELOFORD	1961	M A STOTESBURY	1990	M SHELDON
1927	H LEAK	1962	R R BARWICK	1991	M SHELDON
1928	J B LIEBERT	1963	M A STOTESBURY	1992	M SHELDON
1929	J B LIEBERT	1964	M A STOTESBURY	1993	M SHELDON
1930	H LEAK	1965	P S ELLISDON	1994	T WADE
1931	H LEAK	1966	M A STOTESBURY	1995	M SHELDON
1932	G W LEDGER	1967	M A STOTESBURY	1996	M SHELDON
1933	G W LEDGER	1968	M A STOTESBURY	1997	L CRANE
1934	G W LEDGER	1969	P S ELLISDON	1998	L CRANE
1935	J R QUERTIER	1970	M A STOTESBURY	1999	M HAYDEN
1936	J R QUERTIER	1971	N R EVANS	2000	B McMANUS
1937	C M O'BRIEN	1972	N R EVANS	2001	B McMANUS
1938	H F CHILTON	1973	N R EVANS	2002	M HAYDEN
1939	B PARKES	1974	N R EVANS	2003	J BARNETT
1940	G MOUNTAIN	1975	N R EVANS	2004	J BARNETT
1946	W E FREEMAN	1976	N R EVANS	2005	J BARNETT
1947	L J CRIDLAND	1977	N R EVANS	2006	N ISA
1948	C M O'BRIEN	1978	A J RICHARDSON	2007	J BARNETT
1949	J R BEST	1979	P J COLEY	2008	J BARNETT
1950	G A MORTON	1980	N R EVANS	2009	R MATHIESON
1951	G G GUNTRIP	1981	P J COLEY	2010	M SHORT
1952	J R BEST				

Singles competitions were played in 1940 but otherwise no tournaments were played 1940–1945 inclusive. Other gaps indicate information unavailable.

Appendix B

Women's Singles Tennis Champions   1911–2010

Year	Champion	Year	Champion	Year	Champion
1914	Mrs E DAVEY	1951	Miss P S F SMITH	1981	Mrs E TAPLIN
1919	Mrs CHADWICK	1952	Miss P S F SMITH	1982	Mrs E TAPLIN
1920	Mrs CHADWICK	1953	Miss P A J SMITH	1983	Mrs E TAPLIN
1921	Miss PENMAN	1954	Miss W M WYER	1984	Mrs E TAPLIN
1922	Miss E M WARD	1955	Miss W M WYER	1985	Miss T PROCTOR
1923	Miss B HISCOX	1956	Miss W M WYER	1986	Miss J R LAW
1924	Mrs H T VODDEN	1957	Miss W M WYER	1987	Miss J R LAW
1925	Mrs H T VODDEN	1958	Miss W M WYER	1988	Mrs E TAPLIN
1926	Mrs H T VODDEN	1959	Miss J A WATTS	1989	Miss M BELLAMY
1927	Miss E M WARD	1960	Miss J McINTOSH	1990	Miss J A BLYTH-LEWIS
1928	Miss M LAYMAN	1961	Miss S J BALDWIN	1991	Miss J ILIFFE
1929	Miss B J CHILTON	1962	Miss J McINTOSH	1992	Miss J ILIFFE
1930	Miss P WHEELER	1963	Miss P J RHODES	1993	Miss L J MOREN
1931	Miss P WHEELER	1964	Miss J L CRIDLAND	1994	Miss L J MOREN
1932	Miss P WHEELER	1965	Miss J L CRIDLAND	1995	Miss L J MOREN
1933	Miss P WHEELER	1966	Miss S J BALDWIN	1996	Miss L J MOREN
1934	Miss E DAVEY	1967	Miss A R FRASER BLACK	1997	Miss C MALYON
1935	Miss M S MacKENZIE	1968	Miss S J BLADWIN	1998	Mrs H LINDFIELD
1936	Miss M WALKER	1969	Mrs S J POSTLETHWAITE	1999	Mrs H LINDFIELD
1937	Miss A WILLSHER	1970	Miss A R FRASER BLACK	2000	Miss Z TWIDLE
1938	Miss M S MacKENZIE	1971	Miss C CLOKE	2001	Miss Z TWIDLE
1939	Miss J QUERTIER	1972	Mrs S J POSTLETHWAITE	2002	Miss Z TWIDLE
1940	Miss J QUERTIER	1973	Miss A R FRASER BLACK	2003	Miss P COATES
1946	Miss P WHEELER	1974	Miss A R FRASER BLACK	2004	Miss Z TWIDLE
1947	Miss P WHEELER	1975	Miss A R FRASER BLACK	2005	Miss Z TWIDLE
1948	Miss P WHEELER	1976	Mrs S J POSTLETHWAITE	2006	Miss Z TWIDLE
1949	Mrs B S K RAMSDEN	1977	Miss M A WHEELER	2007	Miss Z TWIDLE
1950	Mrs B S K RAMSDEN	1978	Miss S E REEVES	2008	Miss E ASHWORTH
		1979	Miss A N CROFT	2009	Miss K BARNETT
		1980	Miss M F WHEELER	2010	Miss R FINCH

Singles competitions were played in 1940 but otherwise no tournaments were played 1940–1945 inclusive. Other gaps indicate information unavailable.

Appendix C

Men's Tennis Doubles Champions   1911–2010

1927	F D GOODCHILD & LEAK	1973	N R EVANS & J JUDSON
1932	H F CHILTON & R E OSBORNE	1974	N R EVANS & J JUDSON
1933	L SHINER & D F STOTESBURY	1975	P S ELLISDON & M O'NEILL
1934	L SHINER & D F STOTESBURY	1976	M STOTESBURY & P D STOTESBURY
1935	HAIGH & S A RAWLINGS	1977	P D STOTESBURY & R TYLER
1936	C M O'BRIEN & J R QUERTIER	1978	P S ELLISDON & M O'NEILL
1937	L SHINER & D F STOTESBURY	1979	J R POTTER & E A THOMPSON
1938	B PARKES & D F STOTESBURY	1980	P S ELLISDON & A J RICHARDSON
1939	L SHINER & D F STOTESBURY	1981	P J COLEY & A J RICHARDSON
1946	P N P BOND & D F STOTESBURY	1982	C J BAILEY & P S ELLISDON
1947	J R BEST & L J CRIDLAND	1983	G E G GERMANY & A J RICHARDSON
1948	C M O'BRIEN & H C O'NEILL	1984	K JACKSON & A RICHARDSON
1949	J R BEST & C M O'BRIEN	1985	J R POTTER & E A THOMPSON
1950	BURTWISTLE & D F STOTESBURY	1986	J R POTTER & E A THOMPSON
1951	J R BEST & C M O'BRIEN	1987	M SHELDON & L DAVIES
1952	G G GUNTRIP & D F STOTESBURY	1992	K G JACKSON & A WELCH
1953	L J CRIDLAND & M F RUTHEN	1993	K G JACKSON & A WELCH
1954	L J CRIDLAND & C M O'BRIEN	1994	K G JACKSON & A WELCH
1955	J R BEST & M F RUTHEN	1995	C JAMES & M SHELDON
1956	L J CRIDLAND & C HAYLOCK	1996	D DRAKE & M HAYDON
1957	C HAYLOCK & M F RUTHEN	1997	D DRAKE & M HAYDON
1958	L J CRIDLAND & C M O'BRIEN	1998	G WAYMAN & R WAYMAN
1959	W H FOORD & M F RUTHEN	1999	H BUSHNELL & T WADE
1960	G G GUNTRIP & B P PEMBRO	2000	D MUSTARD & K DEWICK
1961	M STOTESBURY & P D STOTESBURY	2001	S VANCE & M HAYDEN
1962	C J BAILEY & R R BARWICK	2002	C MASON & M SHELDON
1963	M STOTESBURY & P D STOTESBURY	2003	J BARNETT & M HAYDON
1964	M STOTESBURY & P D STOTESBURY	2004	K DEWICK & M SHELDON
1965	M STOTESBURY & P D STOTESBURY	2005	M ILLINGWORTH & J LANGFORD
1966	M STOTESBURY & P D STOTESBURY	2006	N ISA & F TARIQUE
1967	M STOTESBURY & P D STOTESBURY	2007	K DEWICK & M SHELDON
1968	P S ELLISDON & K J GROVES	2008	N ISA & F SARGEANT
1969	M STOTESBURY & P D STOTESBURY	2009	N ISA & L CRANE
1972	M STOTESBURY & P D STOTESBURY	2010	R MATHIESON & M SHELDON

Singles competitions were played in 1940 but otherwise no tournaments were played 1940–1945 inclusive. Other gaps indicate information unavailable.

Appendix D

Women's Tennis Doubles Champions 1911–2010

1927	MRS D KNOOP & MRS H T VODDEN
1932	MISS M LAYMAN & MISS P WHEELER
1933	MISS M LAYMAN & MISS P WHEELER
1934	MISS E DAVEY & MISS E MARLER
1935	MISS M LAYMAN & MISS P WHEELER
1936	MRS DANE & MISS M WALKER
1937	MISS L MACKENZIE & MISS M MACKENZIE
1938	MISS L MACKENZIE & MISS M MACKENZIE
1939	MISS L MACKENZIE & MISS M MACKENZIE
1946	MISS L MACKENZIE & MRS M S TWINN
1947	MISS M J LOTTIN & MISS F WEST
1948	MRS E M CRIDLAND & MISS A WILLSHER
1949	MISS P A J SMITH & MISS P S F SMITH
1950	MISS P A J SMITH & MISS P S F SMITH
1951	MISS P A J SMITH & MISS P S F SMITH
1952	MISS P A J SMITH & MISS P S F SMITH
1953	MRS B S K RAMSDEN & MISS W M WYER
1954	MISS Z E URMSTON & MISS W M WYER
1955	MISS Z E URMSTON & MISS W M WYER
1956	MISS Z E URMSTON & MISS W M WYER
1957	MISS Z E URMSTON & MISS W M WYER
1958	MISS M J LOTTIN & MISS W M WYER

Singles competitions were played in 1940 but otherwise no tournaments were played 1940–1945 inclusive. Other gaps indicate information unavailable.

1959	MISS M J LOTTIN & MISS J A WATTS
1960	MISS M PARKINSON & MRS B RAMSDEN
1961	MISS S J BALDWIN & MISS J BROCKINGTON
1962	MISS S J BALDWIN & MISS J BROCKINGTON
1963	MISS J CRIDLAND & MISS A FRASER BLACK
1964	MISS J CRIDLAND & MISS A FRASER BLACK
1965	MISS S J BALDWIN & MISS Z URMSTON
1966	MISS S J BALDWIN & MISS Z URMSTON
1967	MISS J CRIDLAND & MISS A FRASER BLACK
1968	MISS J CRIDLAND & MISS A FRASER BLACK
1969	MISS J CRIDLAND & MISS A FRASER BLACK
1970	MISS A FRASER BLACK & MRS J WILLIAMS
1971	MISS A FRASER BLACK & MRS J WILLIAMS
1972	MRS S J POSTLETHWAITE & MISS Z URMSTON
1973	MISS A FRASER BLACK & MRS J WILLIAMS
1974	MISS A FRASER BLACK & MRS J WILLIAMS
1975	MISS A FRASER BLACK & MRS J WILLIAMS
1976	MISS A FRASER BLACK & MRS J WILLIAMS
1977	MISS A FRASER BLACK & MRS J WILLIAMS
1978	MISS A FRASER BLACK & MRS J WILLIAMS
1979	MISS A FRASER BLACK & MRS J WILLIAMS
1980	MISS A FRASER BLACK & MRS J WILLIAMS
1981	MISS J M REEVES & MISS M F WHEELER
1982	MRS S L HONEY & MRS E TAPLIN
1983	MRS S L HONEY & MRS E TAPLIN
1992	MISS C LAMING & MISS J ILIFFE
1993	MISS L MOREN & MRS J MCCONVILLE
1994	MISS L MOREN & M WHEELER
1997	JANE WALMSLEY & C MALYON
1998	H LINFIELD & Z TWIDLE
1999	C LAMING & J STOTESBURY
2000	H LINFIELD & Z TWIDLE
2001	S BAMFORD & S WILLIAMS
2003	V ROWE & G ALLEN
2004	C MALYON & ZOE TWIDLE
2005	C MALYON & ZOE TWIDLE
2006	G ALLEN & JANE BOFFA
2007	K BARNETT & H READ
2008	K BARNETT & E ASHWORTH
2009	S BOTHAM & R FINCH
2010	S BOTHAM & R FINCH

Appendix E

Leading Badminton Players at Parklangley

Internationals

Name	Years Active	Appearances
John Best	1952-60	34
Audrey Dance (née Stone)	1954-66	3
Heather Guntrip (née Parfitt)		1
Nick Yates[1]	1979-88	105

[1] Nick was a member for only a short time but did much of his training at the Club

County Colours

Name	Years Active
Mrs. K. Burgess Smith	1928/29
Audrey Dance (née Stone)	1946/47
Barbara Kitton	1947/48
John Best	1950/51
Heather Guntrip (née Parfitt)	1953/54
Stephen Woodley[2]	1964/65
David Smith	1966/67
Nicholas Yates[2]	1979/80
Hugh Elsdood	1984/85
Joanna Muggeridge[2]	1985/86

[2] Member of Parklangley for only a short time

County Half Colours

Name	Years Active
R.S. Lucas	1947/48
John Kemp	1952/53
Pauline Lawrence	1956/57
Stephanie Postlethwaite (née Baldwin)	1958/59
Cathy Buck	1969/70
Mary Benfield	1982/83
Ian Cameron	1989/90
Danny Horrigan	1989/90

County Second Team Colours

Name	Years Active
Lesley Mackenzie	1946/47
Alice Wilsher	1946/47
Eileen Stotesbury (née Davey)	1947/48
Joy O'Brien (née Prebble)	1948/49
Graham Lawrence	1958/59
Graham Iliffe	1970/71
Penny Forrest	1976/77
David Easterby	1977/78
Mary Benfield	1981/82
Jonathan Smith	1983/84
Linda Pilkington (née Powell)	1984/85
Neil Foxwell	1987/88

County Third Team Colours

Name	Years Active
Barry Amos	1959/60
Paul Gerrard	1959/60
Mary Sands	1961/62
Lesley Iliffe (née Corney)	1965/66
Chris D'Souza	1966/67
Graham Williams	1970/71
Rodney Forrest	1971/72
Michael Howes	1972/73
Chris Mullender	1977/78
Linda Pilkington (née Powell)	1983/84
Susan Peek	1984/85
Kathy Marshall	1984/85
Julie Foxwell	1986/87

Successes (tournaments won)

John Best	All England Championships	Mixed Doubles 1954
	English Invitation	Men's Doubles 1954/55, 1958/59
		Mixed Doubles 1954/55, 1955/56, 1956/57
	Kent Open	Men's Doubles 5 times
		Mixed Doubles 4 times
	Kent Restricted	Men's Singles 5 times
		Men's Doubles 5 times
		Mixed Doubles 9 times running

Audrey Stone[3]	French Open	Ladies' Singles 1952
		Ladies' Doubles 1948, 1949, 1951, 1952, 1960
		Mixed Doubles 1950 with Eddy Chang
	English Invitation	Ladies' Singles 1954/55
		Ladies' Doubles 1954/55
		Mixed Doubles 1954/55
	Kent Open	Mixed Doubles 4 times
	Kent Restricted	Ladies' Singles 6 times
		Ladies' Doubles 6 times
		Mixed Doubles 7 times running

[3] Audrey Stone's England International blazer is on show at the Badminton England Museum in Milton Keynes

Heather Guntrip	Kent Restricted	Ladies' Singles once
		Ladies' Doubles twice
		Mixed Doubles once
Pauline Lawrence	Kent Restricted	Ladies' Singles once
		Ladies' Doubles twice
David Smith	Kent Restricted	Men's Doubles once

Nick Yates	World Championships Team	1983, 1985, 1987
	European Championships Team	1980, 1982, 1984
		1982 won Bronze Medal Men's Singles
	Commonwealth Games	1982 won Silver Medal Men's Singles and Doubles
		1986 won Team Championship, Bronze Men's Singles
	Grand Prix Finals Tokyo	1985 reached finals
	Japan Open	1988 Men's Singles

| Mary Benfield | All England | Veteran Ladies' Doubles Champion |
| | Devon Open | Ladies' Doubles Champion |

1958/59 & 1959/60 Parklangley First teams won Men's, Ladies' and Mixed Division 1 in Kent.

Parklangley Ladies' First Team won 1st Division in Kent eight years running from 1957/58 to 1964/65.

Parklangley Mixed First team won 1st Division Kent in 1958/59, 1959/60, 1963/64 and 1964/65.

A regular Kent and England player, Paul Whetnall was Parklangley's Club Coach for several years and, during his time with them, won the Commonwealth Games Veterans Singles.

Rod Forrest, Mary Benfield and Marian McKelvie have all played for Kent Veterans and have won National Championships in their age groups.

In more recent times Richard Sayers and Sarah King have played for the Kent First team and the following members have played for the Second or Third teams: John Currie, David Currie, Mike Murray, Lindsay Arrowsmith, Steve Thorn, Matt Hilcock, John Brown, Nicci Garner, Clare Small, Luke Green, Faye Garner, Lawrence Nemosthy, Neil Clements.

Appendix F

Men's Squash Champions

1975	David Manning	1993	Graeme White
1976	David Manning	1994	Mark Sheldon
1977	David Manning	1995	Graeme White
1978	David Manning	1996	David Manning
1979	David Manning	1997	David Manning
1980	*unknown*	1998	David Manning
1981	*unknown*	1999	Clive London
1982	Alan Rich	2000	Lee Wilson
1983	Mike Burdon-Taylor	2001	Clive London
1984	Graham Jordon	2002	David Harris
1985	Mike Burdon-Taylor	2003	Clive London
1986	Graham Jordon	2004	Clive London
1987	Graham Jordon	2005	Steve London
1988	Graham Jordon	2006	Steve London
1989	Graham Jordon	2007	Ted Jeal
1990	Graham Jordon	2008	Ted Jeal
1991	Chris Fink	2009	Clive London
1992	**Roy Robson**	2010	Steve London

Bibliography

[1] Watkins and Manning. *Beckenham: The Home Front.* Jenna Publishing, 2005.

[2] S Finch. *Beckenham and West Wickham.* Tempus Publishing Ltd., 2003.

[3] Macdonald. *The History of the Parklangley Golf Club 1910 – 1985.* published privately by Langley Park Golf Club Ltd., 1985.

[4] H. Rob Copeland. *The Village of Old Beckenham.* ORMA Publishing, 2004.

[5] W Knoop. *Parklangley Lawn Tennis and Badminton Club – Memories on the occasion of The Golden Jubilee 1911-1961.* 1961.

[6] Various. *The Parklangley Club 75th Anniversary Celebrations.* 1986.

[7] Ian Crane. *Parklangley Tennis Club Tournaments up to 1983.* 1984.

The Inner Space Work Book By Cat Summers & Julian Vayne

A detailed, practical book on psychic and personal development using the Tarot, pathworkings and meditations. The Inner Space Work Book provides a framework for developing your psychic and magickal abilities; exploring techniques as varied as shamanism, bodymind skills and ritual, through the medium of the tarot. There are two interwoven pathways through the text. One concentrates on the development of psychic sensitivity, divination and counselling, as well as discussing their ethics and practical application. The second pathway leads the student deeper into the realm of Inner Space, exploring the Self through meditation, pathworking, physical exercises and ritual. Both paths weave together to provide the student with a firm grounding in many aspects of the esoteric. Together, the pathways in The Inner Space Work Book, form a 'user friendly' system for unlocking all your latent magickal talents.

ISBN 1 898307 13 X   Price £9.95

Pathworking 2nd Ed. By Pete Jennings & Pete Sawyer

A pathworking is, very simply, a guided meditational exercise, it is sometimes referred to as 'channelling' or 'questing'. It is used for many different aims, from raising consciousness to healing rituals You don't have to possess particular beliefs or large sums of money to benefit from it & it can be conducted within a group or solo at time intervals to suit you. This book teaches you how to alter your conscious state, deal with stress, search for esoteric knowledge or simply have fun & relax. It starts with a clear explanation of the theory of pathworking and shows in simple & concise terms what it is about and how to achieve results, then goes on to more advanced paths & how to develop your own, it also contains over 30 detailed and explained pathworkings. Highly practical advice & information is given on how to establish and manage your own group. No previous experience is assumed.

ISBN Number   1 898307 00 8   Price £7.95

Celtic Lore & Druidic Ritual By Rhiannon Ryall

Rhiannon Ryall is well known for her book 'West Country Wicca'. This new book brings some of the inner mysteries to those interested in the Pagan Path or Tradition. Inevitably the Druidic Path crosses that of any genuine Gaelic Tradition of Wicca, so this book contains much druidic lore.. Background material pertaining to the Druids is also included as this explains much of their way of viewing the world and it enables the reader to understand more fully their attributions in general and their rituals in particular. The book is divided into five parts:

1: Casting circles, seasonal sigils, wands, woods for times of the year, Celtic runes, the Great Tides, making cones and vortices, polarities and how to change them, the seasonal Ogham keys and some Ogham correspondences. 2: Old calendar festivals and associated evocations, the "Call of Nine", two versions of the 'Six pointed Star Dance', Mistletoe Lore, New Moon working,the Fivefold Calendar. 3: Underlying fundamentals of magical work, magical squares and their applications, more use of Oghams, the Diamond Working area. 4: Five initiations, including a shamanic one, some minor 'calls', some 'little magics'. 5: Background information on the Celtic path, the Arthurian myth and its underlying meaning and significance, the Three Worlds of the Celts, thoughts regarding the Hidden Path, some thoughts and final advice. A veritable treasure trove for anyone interested in the Celtic path.

ISBN 1 898307 225   Price £9.95

Angels & Goddesses - Celtic Paganism & Christianity
by Michael Howard

This book traces the history and development of Celtic Paganism and Celtic Christianity specifically in Wales, but also in relation to the rest of the British Isles including Ireland, during the period from the Iron Age, through to the present day. It also studies the transition between the old pagan religions & Christianity & how the early Church, especially in the Celtic counmtries, both struggled with & later absorbed the earlier forms of spirituality it encountered. The book also deals with the way in which the Roman Catholic version of Christianity arrived in south-east England & the end of the 6th century, when the Pope sent St. Augustine on his famous mission to convert the pagan Saxons, & how this affected the Celtic Church.. It discusses how the Roman Church suppressed Celtic Christianity & the effect this was to have on the history & theology of the Church during the later Middle Ages. The influence of Celtic Chhristianity on the Arthurian legends & the Grail romances is explored as well as surviving traditions of Celtic bardism in the medieval period. The conclusion on the book covers the interest in Celtic Christianity today & how, despite attempts to eradicate it from the pages of clerical history, its ideas & ideals have managed to survive & are now influencing New Age concepts & are relevent to the critical debate about the future of the modern chrurch.

ISBN 1-898307-03-2   Price £9.95

Auguries and Omens - The Magical Lore of Birds   By Yvonne Aburrow

The folklore & mythology of birds is central to an understanding of the ancient world, yet it is a neglected topic. This book sets out to remedy this situation, examining in detail the interpretation of birds as auguries & omens, the mythology of birds (Roman, Greek, Celtic & Teutonic), the folklore & weather lore associated with them, their use in heraldry & falconry & their appearances in folk songs & poetry. The book examines these areas in a general way, then goes into specific details of individual birds from the albatross to the yellowhammer, including many indigenous British species, as well as more exotic & even mythical birds.

ISBN Number 1 898307 11 3   Price £10.95

The Pickingill Papers - The Origin of the Gardnerian Craft by W. E. Liddell
Compiled & Edited by Michael Howard

George Pickingill (1816 - 1909) was said to be the leader of the witches in Canewdon, Essex. In detailed correspondence with 'The Wiccan' & 'The Cauldron' magazines from 1974 - 1994, E. W. Liddell, claimed to be a member of the 'true persuasion', i.e. the Hereditary Craft. He further claimed that he had relatives in various parts of southern England who were coven leaders & that his own parent coven (in Essex) had been founded by George Pickingill's grandfather in the 18th century. There is considerable interest in the material in the so-called 'Pickingill Papers' & the controversy still rages about their content & significance with regard to the origins of Gardnerian Wicca. This book provides, for the first time, a chance for the complete Pickingill material to be read & examined in toto together with background references & extensive explanatory notes. Topics included in this book include the origin of the Gardnerian Book of Shadows and Aleister Crowley's involvement, the relationship between the Hereditary Craft, Gardnerian Wicca & Pickingill's Nine Covens, the influence of Freemasonry on the medieval witch cult, sex magic, ley lines & earth energy, prehistoric shamanism, the East Anglian lodges of cunning men, the difference between Celtic wise women & the Anglo Saxon cunning men. It also includes new material on the Craft Laws, the New Forest coven, Pickingill's influence on the Revived Craft & a refutation of the material on Lugh & his basic thesis in Aidan Kelly's recent book 'Crafting the Art of Magic'.

ISBN Number 1 898307 10 5   Price £9.95

A selection of other titles from Capall Bann:

Available through your local bookshop, or direct from Capall Bann at:
Freshfields, Chieveley, Berks, RG16 8TF.

West Country Wicca - A Journal of the Old Religion By Rhiannon Ryall

This book is a valuable and enjoyable contribution to contemporary Wicca. It is a simple account of the Old Religion. The portrayal of Wicca in the olden days is at once charming and deeply religious, combining joy, simplicity and reverence. The wisdom emanating from country folk who live close to Nature shines forth from every page - a wisdom which can add depth and colour to our present day understanding of the Craft. Without placing more value on her way than ours, Rhiannon provides us with a direct path back to the Old Religion in the British Isles. *This is how it was*, she tells us. *This is the way I remember it.* Both the content of what she remembers and the form in which she tells us, are straightforward, homespun and thoroughly unaffected.

"West Country Wicca is a real gem - it is the best book on witchcraft I have ever seen! Thank you Rhiannon Ryall for sharing your path with us." - Marion Weinstein

ISBN Number   1 89830 702 4   Price £7.95

The Call of the Horned Piper by Nigel Aldcroft Jackson

This book originated as a series of articles, later much expanded, covering the symbolism, archetypes and myths of the Traditional Craft (or Old Religion) in the British Isles and Europe. The first section of the book explores the inner symbology and mythopoetics of the old Witchraft religion, whilst the second part gives a practical treatment of the sacred sabbatic cycle, the working tools, incantations, spells and pathworking. There are also sections on spirit lines, knots and thread lore and ancestral faery teachings. Extensively illustrated with the author's original artwork. This is a radical and fresh re-appraisal of authentic witch-lore which may provide a working alternative to current mainstream trends in Wicca.

ISBN Number   1-898307-09-1   Price £8.95

The Sacred Grove - The Mysteries of the Tree By Yvonne Aburrow

The veneration of trees was a predominant theme in the paganism of the Romans, Greeks, Celtic & Germanic peoples. Many of their rites took place in sacred groves & much of their symbolism involved the cosmic tree; its branches supported the heavens, its trunk was the centre of the earth & its roots penetrated the underworld. This book explains the various mysteries of the tree & explains how these can be incorporated into modern paganism. This gives a new perspective on the cycle of seasonal festivals & the book includes a series of rituals incorporating tree symbolism. "The Sacred Grove" is the companion volume to "The Enchanted Forest - The Magical Lore of Trees, but can be read in its own right as an exploration of the mysteries of the tree.

ISBN Number 1 898307 12 1   Price £10.95

EUROPE

DALRIADA, Dun-na-Beatha, 2 Brathwic Place, Brodick, Isle of Arran, KA27 8BN, Scotland

STARLIGHT, PO Box 452, 00101 Helsinki, Finland.

TALKING STICK, 117 Coteford Street, London SW17 8MX

THE CAULDRON, Mike Howard, Caemorgan Cottage, Caemorgan Road, Cardigan, Dyfed SA43 1QU, Wales (NB: Do not put "THE CAULDRON" on the envelope)

THE WICCAN, BM Box 7097, London WC1N 3XX (Journal of The PAGAN FEDERATION)

WEB OF WYRD, BM Box 9290, London WC1N 3XX

WICCAN REDE, PO Box 473, NL-3700-Al Zeist, Netherlands